CBA CHRISTIAN BAUER

ULF MEYER

Edited by Falk Jaeger
Photographs by Lukas Roth

JOVIS

PORTFOLIO

CBA CHRISTIAN BAUER

ULF MEYER

Edited by Falk Jaeger
Photographs by Lukas Roth

JOVIS

Alle vorgestellten Projekte sind mit Koordinaten versehen, die es erlauben, die Standorte der Gebäude z.B. über GoogleEarth exakt zu lokalisieren. For all projects presented coordinates are provided allowing the exact localisation of the buildings via GoogleEarth or other applications. © 2010 by jovis Verlag GmbH I Das Copyright für die Texte liegt beim Autor. Das Copyright für die Abbildungen liegt bei den Fotografen/Inhabern der Bildrechte. Texts by kind permission of the author. Pictures by kind permission of the photographers/holders of the picture rights. Die Gesamtreihe Portfolio wird herausgegeben von Falk Jaeger The series Portfolio is edited by Falk Jaeger I Umschlagfoto Cover: Lukas Roth I Alle Renderings, Zeichnungen, Abbildungen und Pläne sind von cba All renderings, sketches, illustrations and drawings cba I Fotos Photographs: Lukas Roth außer except cba 16 (r.), 17, 18 (m., r.), 20 (two pictures r.), 154–157, 159 I Clemens Ortmeyer 42–47 I Guy Wolff 120/121 I Andres Lejona 151 I Mao Meyer 158 I Alle Rechte vorbehalten. All rights reserved. I Übersetzung Translation: englisch english: Julian Jain, Berlin französisch french: Chantal Pradines, Ingénieur Centrale Paris, F-88350 Trampot I Gestaltung und Satz Design and setting: Susanne Rösler, Berlin I Lithografie Lithography: Bild1Druck, Berlin I Druck und Bindung Printing and binding: GCC Grafisches Centrum Cuno, Calbe I Bibliografische Information der Deutschen Nationalbibliothek Bibliographic information published by Die Deutsche Nationalbibliothek Die Deutsche Nationalbibliothek verzeichnet diese Publikation in der Deutschen Nationalbibliografie; detaillierte bibliografische Daten sind im Internet über http://dnb.d-nb. de abrufbar. Die Deutsche Nationalbibliothek lists this publication in the Deutsche Nationalbibliografie; detailed bibliographic data are available in the Internet at http://dnb.d-nb.de jovis Verlag GmbH I Kurfürstenstraße 15/16 I 10785 Berlin I www.jovis.de I ISBN 978-3-86859-036-4

CONTENTS

FOREWORD

PRÉFACE
VORWORT

Falk Jaeger

Luxembourg is a fascinating place indeed. The country is keenly aware of its cherished traditions and historical values while it excels at being open and globalized, with Luxembourgers being true citizens of the world. While Luxembourg's topographically, economically and politically central situation in the heart of Europe is impressive, to none more so than the French. In Germany, Luxembourg is admired for its close and forthright relationship with France. Furthermore, Luxembourg's mediating role between the neighbors has shaped the country over the last few decades. Architecture stood to benefit from this situation. Luxembourg regularly appears on the itineraries of architecture tourists who are out to visit new, pioneering buildings in the country.

It was this environment that has considerably shaped the Luxembourg architect Christian Bauer though it was in Zurich that he completed his architecture studies. Luxembourg's situation is clearly reflected in his work. The portfolio of the cba office's work encompasses a wide range of building typologies, from villas snugly embedded into a landscape, serving as Luxembourgers' private retreats, to public buildings such as the European School on the Kirchberg, located at the country's international cultural, financial and political center. Other examples include an engineering firm's office which has been lovingly integrated into a historical courtyard setting and the spacious headquarters of a firm specializing in communication satellite systems.

Un lieu fascinant, ce Luxembourg. Soucieux de tradition et attachés aux valeurs, les Luxembourgeois se glissent cependant avec aisance dans le rôle de fringants citoyens du monde. La position centrale du pays, au cœur de l'Europe – topographiquement, économiquement et surtout politiquement –, impressionne les Français tandis que d'Allemagne, on admire la relation étroite et toute naturelle du Luxembourg avec la France. Au cours des dernières décennies, le rôle de médiateur entre pays voisins a ainsi façonné le Luxembourg. L'architecture en a tiré bénéfice : le Luxembourg ne cesse de s'imposer sur les circuits du tourisme architectural dès lors qu'il s'agit de visiter des constructions modernes, novatrices.

C'est dans cet environnement que l'architecte luxembourgeois Christian Bauer s'est construit, personnellement et – en dépit d'une formation à Zurich – en tant qu'architecte. Ceci se reflète dans son travail. Le portfolio du bureau cba balaie ainsi une œuvre où les deux extrêmes sont présents : d'un côté la villa dissimulée, retraite intime du Luxembourgeois, de l'autre l'École européenne sur le plateau du Kirchberg, au cœur même du réseau culturel, financier et politique international du pays. Ou encore le cabinet d'ingénierie délicatement inséré dans son arrière-cour historique et son pendant, le siège d'une société de satellites de communication, bâtiment d'envergure planté au large, visant en quelque sorte les hautes sphères.

Ein faszinierender Standort, dieses Luxemburg. Einerseits traditionsbewusst und wertkonservativ geprägt, schlüpfen die Luxemburger dennoch mit Leichtigkeit in die Rolle des gewandten Weltbürgers. Die Franzosen beeindruckt die topografisch, wirtschaftlich und vor allem politisch zentrale Situation Luxemburgs inmitten Europas. Von Deutschland aus bewundert man sicher Luxemburgs enge und ganz selbstverständliche Beziehung zu Frankreich. Darüber hinaus bestimmte die Mittlerrolle zwischen den Nachbarländern das Land in den vergangenen Jahrzehnten. Die Architektur hat daraus Vorteile gezogen. Luxemburg scheint immer wieder auf der Landkarte der Architekturtouristen auf, wenn es gilt, neueste, wegweisende Bauten zu besuchen.

Der Luxemburger Architekt Christian Bauer hat in diesem Umfeld seine Sozialisierung und – trotz Ausbildung in Zürich – architektonische Prägung erfahren. In seiner Arbeit spiegelt sich diese Situation wider. Im Portfolio des Büros cba finden sich beide Extreme als Bauaufgabe: die versteckte Villa als privater Rückzugsort des Luxembourgeois genauso wie die Europaschule auf dem Luxemburger Kirchberg, unmittelbar im Brennpunkt des internationalen Kultur-, Finanz- und Politiknetzwerks des Landes. Oder auch das geradezu liebevoll in seine historische Hinterhofsituation eingepasste Ingenieurbüro einerseits und andererseits die raumgreifende Hauptverwaltung eines Kommunikationssatellitensystems auf wei-

While many architects at the end of the nineteen-eighties saw the period of postmodernism as something that needed to be overcome as quickly as possible, Christian Bauer took inspiration from it, with the ideas of Robert Venturi and of the Krier brothers from Luxembourg shaping him in particular. Postmodernism's original goal, i.e. to complement and not replace modernism which had stiffened into a kind of "economic functionalism," still remains a worthy objective. The plan was to add certain elements to it which were perceived to be missing, such as symbolism, meaning, expression and a sense of atmosphere, and integrate them into a re-emerged modern architectural language. Similarly, the achievements of postmodern urban planning which stressed issues of urban density and the typological richness of the European city continue to inspire the architects at cba, much in contrast to Le Corbusier's rigid CIAM maxims.

This JOVIS PORTFOLIO charts the course of Christian Bauer and his team on their way to creating a new Luxembourg shaped by *savoir vivre*, sociability and openness which finds expression in architecture.

Tandis qu'à la fin des années quatre-vingts, nombre d'architectes voyaient dans l'ère postmoderne une époque qu'il s'agissait de dépasser au plus vite (pour autant que l'on se sentait concerné), Christian Bauer tirait de la pensée de Robert Venturi et de celle des frères Krier – des Luxembourgeois – les enseignements véritables. De fait, l'objectif initial du post-modernisme – ne pas remplacer un modernisme figé dans un «fonctionnalisme économique», mais le compléter de ce qui lui faisait défaut : symbolique, sens, expression, atmosphère –, demeure valable et peut être atteint en usant du langage architectural moderne redevenu entre temps familier. Et même les réalisations de l'urbanisme postmoderne, qui a remis à l'honneur la densité urbaine et la riche typologie de la ville européenne, constituent pour les architectes de cba des jalons plus fiables que les préceptes des CIAM de Le Corbusier prônant un urbanisme ouvert.

Ce PORTFOLIO jovis suit Christian Bauer et son équipe dans leur parcours vers un Luxembourg nouveau, rompu à l'usage du monde, affable et ouvert et qui exprime cela aussi dans son architecture.

ter Flur und gewissermaßen mit der Orientierung in höhere Sphären.

Während viele Architekten Ende der achtziger Jahre die Zeit der Postmoderne als eine Epoche sahen, die es möglichst rasch zu überwinden galt (so man sich davon überhaupt angesprochen gefühlt hatte), hat Christian Bauer aus der Ideenwelt von Robert Venturi und der (Luxemburger) Gebrüder Krier die richtigen Lehren gezogen. Das ursprüngliche Ziel der Postmoderne, die im „Wirtschaftsfunktionalismus" erstarrte Moderne nicht zu ersetzen, sondern sie um Fehlendes zu erweitern, um Symbolik, Bedeutung, Ausdruck und Atmosphäre, ist ja noch immer ein plausibles Anliegen und kann mit der inzwischen wieder gängigen modernen Architektursprache verfolgt werden. Und selbst die Errungenschaften des postmodernen Städtebaus, der die urbane Dichte und den typologischen Reichtum der europäischen Stadt wieder in Wertschätzung brachte, sind für die Architekten von cba eher Richtschnur als Le Corbusiers CIAM-Leitsätze für den offenen Städtebau.

Dieses JOVIS PORTFOLIO verfolgt Christian Bauer und sein Team auf dem Weg in ein neues Luxemburg, das von Weltgewandtheit, Kontaktfreude und Offenheit geprägt ist und dies auch in der Architektur zum Ausdruck bringt.

WORKING AT THE INTERFACE

TRAVAILLER À L'INTERFACE
ARBEITEN AN DER SCHNITTSTELLE

The Architecture Firm cba's Secret of Success Is Wonderfully Simple The Luxembourger architecture practice of christian bauer & associés architectes (cba) is professional in the positive sense of the word: in contrast to widespread belief in- and outside the profession, the office understands architecture not as being the exclusive creative realm of the architect alone. For Christian Bauer, the founder and eponym of the office, the creative part of a building project does not suffice to translate an idea into built reality with a sustainable existence.

Images are not enough to create true architecture, even if they continue to be a powerful influence. Architects need an understanding of many different issues in order to create good architecture, including art and technology, law and economics, as well as physics and psychology. This transforms the profession of the architect into a permanent challenge while it also constitutes the source of its richness. According to Bauer, if architects again want to become trustworthy, globally responsible partners, they must follow through the process of realizing buildings from beginning to end while relying on themselves. Good architecture, indeed, cannot emerge when a design, creative as it may be, is prematurely handed over to a myopic construction partner. The key to cba's success lies in the fact that it has several different skills and capabilities: apart from building construction expertise, it has competencies in the design of interiors, urban planning, visual communication,

Le succès de cba, un succès extraordinairement simple Professionalisme : tel est le maître-mot du cabinet cba – christian bauer & associés architectes. L'idée qui a présidé à l'existence de cet atelier d'architecture et d'urbanisme luxembourgeois, et qui en a fait le succès, est en effet que l'architecte, contrairement à un point de vue largement répandu, tant dans la profession qu'à l'extérieur de celle-ci, n'est pas un simple créatif. Christian Bauer, le fondateur du cabinet éponyme, est convaincu que la créativité ne suffit pas pour faire d'une idée – abstraite – une construction – concrète, et qui plus est, durable.

L'architecture véritable ne se résume pas à des images, même si celles-ci ont souvent un grand pouvoir. Pour qu'une bonne architecture s'ancre dans la réalité, les architectes doivent toucher à bien des domaines : l'art et la technique, le droit et l'économie, la physique et la psychologie. C'est là à la fois la difficulté de la profession, mais aussi toute sa richesse. Pour Christian Bauer, si les architectes doivent redevenir des partenaires fiables, assumant une responsabilité globale, ils doivent s'impliquer dans leurs projets, de A à Z, jusqu'à leur concrétisation finale. En effet, on ne produit pas de bonne architecture avec un concepteur créatif d'un côté, un technicien spécialiste exclusif de la construction de l'autre, le premier abandonnant au second son projet aux tous premiers stades de l'opération, bien trop tôt, en tout cas. La clé du succès du cabinet de Christian Bauer se trouve justement

Das Erfolgsgeheimnis des Büros cba ist angenehm einfach Das Luxemburger Büro christian bauer & associés architectes (cba) ist im besten Sinne des Wortes professionell: Das Verständnis, das dem erfolgreichen Büro zugrunde liegt, sieht den Architekten – entgegen weitverbreiteter Auffassung inner- und außerhalb des Berufsstandes – nicht allein als Kreativen. Für Christian Bauer, den Gründer und Namensgeber des Büros, genügt der kreative Anteil einer baulichen Schöpfung allein nicht, um der Idee in der Wirklichkeit Bestand zu geben – und damit die Chance auf eine nachhaltige Existenz.

Bilder alleine reichen für wahre Baukunst nicht aus, auch wenn sie oft viel Macht haben. Um gute Architektur Lebenswirklichkeit werden zu lassen, müssen Architekten folglich von vielen Dingen etwas verstehen: von Kunst und Technik, Recht und Wirtschaft, ebenso wie von Physik und Psychologie. Das macht den Beruf des Architekten zu einer ständigen Herausforderung, es macht zugleich aber auch den Reichtum der Profession aus. Wenn Architekten wieder zu verlässlichen, global verantwortlichen Partnern werden sollen, müssen sie – so Bauer – ihre Entwürfe von A bis Z begleiten und bis zum Ende selbst umsetzen. Tatsächlich entsteht gute Baukunst nicht, wenn ein kreativer Entwerfer auf der einen Seite sein Projekt allzu früh einem lediglich mit der Umsetzung vertrauten Partner auf der anderen Seite übergeben muss. Der Schlüssel zum Erfolg des Büros Bauer liegt also darin, verschiedene Fähigkeiten im eigenen Haus zu pflegen:

as well as structural engineering, and landscape design and gardens, where the architects work together with a diverse range of expert planners.

More than once, the good reputation the cba office enjoys in Luxembourg and abroad has led to its participation in partnerships with even more acclaimed architecture firms who often don't have all the required professional capabilities themselves to successfully complete a project. Apart from these kinds of partnerships (such as the one with Christian de Portzamparc from France), there are also others where both partners engage with each other on an equal footing, such as the one with the firm Baumschlager/Eberle from Austria, that also contribute to the international acclaim of the practice.

At Home all around the World Luxembourg is located at a geographical and cultural crossroads between German- and French-speaking regions, giving it the capacity to productively utilize this proximity for its own advancement. Christian Bauer himself is an example of this, with his multi-lingual and sophisticatedly diplomatic personality. He is open towards the world. He also looks beyond Europe and its cultural differences, having traveled the entire world, from the vast expanses of North America to the holy sites of India, from the temple gardens of Japan to the most remote villages of the kingdom of Bhutan, always opening his eyes to both the high, classical art of building and more profane examples of architecture.

là : dans la complémentarité des différentes compétences cultivées en interne – dans le domaine de la construction mais aussi de l'architecture intérieure, de l'urbanisme, de la communication visuelle –, ainsi que dans la collaboration avec des spécialistes de bureaux d'études extérieurs pour l'ingénierie et l'architecture paysagère.

De fait, si cba a été retenu comme partenaire par des cabinets d'architecture éminents mais dans l'impossibilité, souvent, d'aligner des compétences aussi étendues en interne, il le doit à la bonne réputation dont jouit le cabinet au Luxembourg comme à l'étranger. À ce type de partenariats – avec Christian de Portzamparc, pour la France, par exemple – s'en ajoutent d'autres, noués plus sur un pied d'égalité, comme avec le cabinet autrichien Baumschlager Eberle, qui contribuent également au succès et à la renommée internationale de cba.

Citoyens du monde Le Luxembourg, interface géographique et culturelle entre le monde francophone et le monde germanophone, a cultivé l'art d'utiliser cette double proximité de façon féconde. Christian Bauer lui-même, gentleman et diplomate tout à la fois, qui manie les langues avec aisance, en est en quelque sorte le champion. Ouvert au monde, habité par une curiosité qui ne se limite pas, de loin, aux différences culturelles européennes, il a parcouru le monde, depuis les grandes étendues de l'Amérique du Nord jusqu'aux villages les plus reculés du royaume du Bhoutan, en passant par les

Neben der Kompetenz im Hochbau betrifft dies auch die Felder der Innenarchitektur, des Städtebaus und der visuellen Kommunikation sowie des Ingenieurwesens und der Landschafts- und Gartenarchitektur, auf denen die Architekten mit externen Fachplanern zusammenarbeiten.

Tatsächlich hat der gute Ruf, den das Büro cba in Luxemburg und darüber hinaus genießt, mehr als einmal dazu geführt, dass es als Partner von noch prominenteren Architekturbüros engagiert wurde, die diese umfassende Kompetenz oft nicht im eigenen Hause bündeln können. Neben dieser Art von Partnerschaften (wie zum Beispiel mit Christian de Portzamparc aus Frankreich) gibt es aber auch gleichberechtigte Entwurfspartnerschaften (wie mit dem Büro Baumschlager Eberle aus Österreich), die ebenfalls zum Erfolg und damit zum internationalen Renommee des Büros cba beitragen.

Zu Hause in der Welt Luxemburg liegt an einer geografischen und kulturellen Schnittstelle zwischen der deutsch- und der französischsprachigen Welt und hat die Fähigkeit, diese doppelte Nähe produktiv zu nutzen, zu einiger Meisterschaft gebracht. Christian Bauer selbst verkörpert dieses Talent in seiner gewandten, multi-lingualen und diplomatischen Art. Er ist der Welt gegenüber aufgeschlossen, dabei ist seine Neugierde nicht auf Europas kulturelle Differenzen beschränkt. Im Gegenteil: Von den Weiten Nordamerikas über die heiligen Stätten In-

The other four partners of the office come from three different countries. Their diverse cultural backgrounds flow into the work of the office. Even if Luxembourg is closer to France than Germany in many respects, Christian Bauer has little doubt that the country's eastern neighbor sets the standard in terms of construction quality and the transparency of procedures and practices. The office intends to further internationalize its operations in the coming years based on the solid foundation it has built for itself at home. When working on large projects, however, Bauer does still look for partners to reduce his firm's dependability on a single project and to better balance employment in his office. The practice is also concerned with finding a well-calibrated mix between private and public clients.

The high benchmarks the architects have set for themselves in terms of the competencies that are available in their office and the wish to realize projects abroad also means that the firm is compelled to take up larger projects. The current size of around thirty members of staff suits Bauer and guarantees a certain efficacy. This does not, however, exclude the possibility that cba may grow in the coming years. At present, the worldwide economic crisis which has also affected Luxembourg with its strong dependency on the financial and banking sector has dashed hopes of fast office expansion. However, every crisis also implies a chance and Bauer has since long recognized this: he believes that if the current drop in economic growth leads to a reaffirmation of quality urban planning, away from efforts that increasingly fragment city peripheries towards a re-evaluation of inner cities, he would very much welcome it.

The office is involved with almost all building typologies: from villas to social housing, from museums to production facilities and

lieux saints de l'Inde ou les jardins des temples japonais, curieux à la fois de l'architecture sacrée et de l'architecture profane.

Les quatre autres associés du cabinet sont originaires de trois pays différents et leur diversité culturelle nourrit elle aussi le travail de l'équipe. Même si le Luxembourg est à maints égards plus proche de la France que de l'Allemagne, Christian Bauer est convaincu que cette dernière constitue la référence en matière de qualité de la construction et de procédures ouvertes. Au cours des prochaines années, le cabinet souhaiterait renforcer encore sa présence sur la scène internationale, en s'appuyant sur les assises solides établies dans son propre pays. Pour les gros projets, Christian Bauer cherche cependant à s'associer à des partenaires afin de ne pas dépendre d'un projet unique et assurer une meilleure régularité de l'activité. Il recherche également un équilibre entre maîtres d'ouvrages privés et maîtres d'ouvrages publics.

La volonté de disposer d'une palette étendue de compétences internes et la capacité à s'attaquer à des projets à l'étranger imposent un cabinet d'une certaine taille. La situation actuelle, avec une trentaine de collaborateurs, convient bien à Christian Bauer, en même temps qu'elle garantit une puissance d'action dans de nombreux domaines. Pour autant, le cabinet pourrait avantageusement s'étoffer encore un peu au cours des prochaines années. La crise économique mondiale, qui n'a pas épargné le Luxembourg, très dépendant du système bancaire et financier, contrarie pour l'heure une expansion rapide. Mais chaque crise est aussi une chance – et Christian Bauer l'a compris depuis longtemps. Il verrait d'un bon œil le fléchissement actuel de la croissance se traduire par un urbanisme de qualité et un réinvestissement de leurs centres par les

diens, die Tempelgärten in Japan bis zu den entlegensten Dörfern im Königreich Bhutan hat Bauer die Welt bereist und dabei stets ein offenes Auge für die hohe und auch die profane Baukunst bewiesen.

Die vier anderen Partner des Büros kommen aus drei Ländern und ihr vielfältiger kultureller Hintergrund fließt ebenfalls in die Arbeit des Büros ein. Auch wenn Luxemburg in vieler Hinsicht Frankreich näher ist als Deutschland, lässt Bauer keinen Zweifel daran, dass der östliche Nachbar Luxemburgs aus seiner Sicht die Maßstäbe in der Bauqualität und in der Offenheit der Verfahren setzt. In den nächsten Jahren möchte sich das Büro – aufbauend auf der soliden Grundlage, die es sich in seiner Heimat erarbeitet hat – stärker internationalisieren. Bei Großprojekten sucht Bauer dennoch Partner, um die Abhängigkeit von nur einem Projekt vermeiden und die Beschäftigung des Büros besser ausbalancieren zu können. Auch zwischen privaten und öffentlichen Bauherren versucht das Büro eine ausgewogene Mischung zu erreichen.

Mit den hohen Ansprüchen, die die Architekten an In-House-Kompetenzen stellen und der Fähigkeit, Projekte im Ausland zu stemmen, geht ein gewisser Zwang zur Größe einher. Der derzeitige Umfang von ca. 30 Mitarbeitern ist dem Büroinhaber angenehm und gewährleistet eine gewisse Schlagkraft. Das bedeutet aber nicht, dass cba in den nächsten Jahren nicht noch ein wenig weiter wachsen dürfte. Derzeit steht die weltweite Wirtschaftskrise, die auch Luxemburg mit seiner starken Abhängigkeit vom Finanz- und Bankenwesen nicht verschont hat, einer schnellen Expansion im Wege. Aber in jeder Krise liegt auch eine Chance – und die hat Bauer schon lange eruiert: Wenn der derzeitige Wachstumsknick dazu führt, dass qualifizierter Städtebau wieder an Bedeutung

restaurants, from the large scale of urban planning to the smallest building detail. Handling diverse building typologies does represent a certain difficulty but this is also an asset since, finally, good urban planning is and ought to be created by architects who also design buildings. Only they know what kinds of architectural repercussions their urban ideas will have.

The Old and the New When offered the choice between designing a greenfield building or planning for a complex site in the city center, Bauer does not hesitate to choose the latter. Building in the context of existing structures is something he has already done to great acclaim, with his Musée national d'histoire et d'art located in the old part of Luxembourg, designated as a UNESCO world cultural heritage site. Making use of already existing structures not only is ecologically more sensible, it is also more exciting architecturally, allowing the old and the new to engage in a "positive confrontation," according to Bauer. Out of choice, the architect therefore enjoys working in urban contexts that are seen as problematic by others.

Even today, the office benefits from the experience it has gained by building the National Museum of Luxembourg. Working in a sensitive inner-city and historical context has inspired the office when translating the knowledge gained to other projects, such as the design competition for the Place Guillaume in Luxembourg, for the new building of the Jewish Museum in Cologne or, more recently, for the townhouse in the old part of Frankfurt am Main. In recent times, this expertise has also brought the office international acclaim, not only within the competition field, but also in terms of built projects, an example being the Domforum in Osnabrück. The project in Frankfurt am Main in-

villes et les bourgs, aujourd'hui trop tournés vers leurs franges urbaines effilochées.

Cba maîtrise pratiquement tous les types de projets, de la villa cossue au logement social, du musée au restaurant ou aux ateliers de fabrication, de la grande échelle urbaine au plus petit détail de construction. Exercice particulièrement difficile, mais force indéniable, ce zoom formidable se révèle un atout précieux : le meilleur urbanisme est finalement l'œuvre d'architectes qui conçoivent eux-mêmes des bâtiments ; parce qu'eux seuls connaissent les implications architectoniques des concepts urbanistiques qu'ils proposent.

Construire le neuf dans l'ancien Placé devant le choix de participer à un concours en pleine nature ou de travailler sur un terrain « difficile » en vieille ville, Christian Bauer n'hésite pas longtemps. Intervenir dans l'existant, il l'a fait de manière magistrale avec la construction du Musée national d'histoire et d'art dans la vieille ville de Luxembourg, patrimoine mondial de l'UNESCO. Ce fut, d'un avis unanime qu'il partage entièrement, l'une des productions les plus réussies de l'ensemble de son œuvre. Construire dans l'existant ne se justifie pas seulement d'un point de vue écologique, la coexistence du neuf et de l'ancien, la « confrontation positive », comme Christian Bauer l'appelle, fait aussi souvent jaillir des étincelles ; c'est pour cela qu'il se plaît à travailler dans les environnements urbains que d'aucuns qualifieraient de difficiles.

Aujourd'hui encore, cba met à profit l'expérience précieuse acquise lors de la construction du Musée national du Luxembourg : l'insertion sensible en centre-ville, dans un contexte historique, caractérise aussi des projets comme celui du concours de la Place Guillaume à Luxembourg, la construction du

gewinnt und die Städte und Gemeinden ihr Augenmerk vom ausfransenden Stadtrand verstärkt auf die Innenstadt richten, soll das Bauer nur recht sein.

Typologisch beherrscht das Büro fast die ganze Bandbreite der Bauaufgaben: von der Villa zum sozialen Wohnungsbau, vom Museum über eine Fertigungsstätte bis zum Restaurant, vom städtebaulichen Großmaßstab bis zum kleinsten Baudetail. Darin liegt eine besondere Schwierigkeit, aber auch Stärke. Denn der beste Städtebau wird schließlich von Architekten praktiziert, die selber auch Hochbauten entwerfen: Nur sie wissen, welche architektonischen Implikationen ihre städtebaulichen Ideen haben.

Alt und Neu Vor die Wahl gestellt, an einem Wettbewerb für ein Projekt auf der grünen Wiese oder für ein „schwieriges" Altstadtgrundstück teilzunehmen, zögert Bauer nicht lange: Das Bauen im Bestand, wie er es beim Bau des Musée national d'histoire et d'art in der zum UNESCO-Weltkulturerbe zählenden Altstadt Luxemburgs meisterlich praktiziert hat, hat ihm schließlich eines der nach Eigen- und Fremdaussage gleichermaßen erfolgreichsten Werke in seinem Œuvre verschafft. Das Bauen im Bestand ist nicht nur ökologisch sinnvoller, es lassen sich oft auch architektonisch Funken aus dem Nebeneinander von Alt und Neu, der „positiven Konfrontation" wie er es nennt, schlagen. Mit Vorliebe arbeitet Bauer deshalb in einem als schwierig titulierten städtebaulichen Umfeld.

Von den wertvollen Erfahrungen, die das Büro beim Bau des Nationalmuseums von Luxemburg gesammelt hat, profitiert es noch heute: Denn das Thema der sensiblen Einfügung in Innenstädte, in den historischen Kontext, prägt auch Entwürfe wie die für den Wettbewerb an der Place Guillaume

volves designing a structure that covers the excavations in the historical core of the city, thus mediating the historical self-image of this modern city of trade and commerce. In contrast to the row of old and new houses at the market, cba's urban planning concept conceived together with Meurer Architekten envisages following the shape of the lost medieval built-form while restoring and redefining the city using contemporary tools and techniques.

Urban Planning Christian Bauer would like his office to grow moderately in the next few

Musée juif de Cologne ou, plus récemment, la *Stadthaus*, dans la vieille ville de Francfort. Cette expérience est aussi à l'origine d'une récente reconnaissance internationale, non seulement dans les concours mais aussi dans des projets réalisés tels ceux du Forum de la cathédrale à Osnabrück. Concernant le projet de Francfort, il s'agit d'un bâtiment destiné à abriter des fouilles archéologiques dans le cœur historique primitif de la ville. L'enjeu du projet n'est pas des moindres, puisqu'il touche à l'identité historique de cette capitale moderne des affaires : faisant face à la rangée de mai-

in Luxemburg, für den Neubau des Jüdischen Museums in Köln oder zuletzt für das Stadthaus in der Altstadt von Frankfurt am Main. Diese Expertise hat dem Büro in letzter Zeit auch international Anerkennung verschafft – nicht nur in der Wettbewerbsszene, sondern auch durch ganz konkrete, realisierte Bauten wie beispielsweise das Domforum in Osnabrück. Bei dem Projekt in Frankfurt am Main hingegen geht es um die Überbauung von Ausgrabungen in der historischen Keimzelle der Stadt, also um nichts weniger als das geschichtliche Selbstverständnis dieser modernen Handelsstadt.

COMPETITION "CENTRE GUILLAUME II," LUXEMBOURG (L), SECOND PRIZE | NATIONAL MUSEUM OF HISTORY AND ART, LUXEMBOURG (L)

years, and in the fields of both urban planning and architecture. He says he is lucky to have had the opportunity to become an advisor for Luxembourg's most significant urban development project, the Kirchberg Plateau. He has followed its rapid growth and problems over the course of many years. The Kirchberg Plateau is Luxembourg's model urban quarter, housing almost all of its institutions and banks that have made the country internationally prominent and given it above-average wealth. This urban quarter, initially laid out according to the

sons anciennes (reconstruites) qui borde le marché, la proposition de cba et de Meurer Architekten reprend la volumétrie du bâti médiéval disparu, tout en s'attachant, avec les moyens contemporains, à réparer et redéfinir la ville.

Urbanisme Christian Bauer souhaiterait voir son cabinet renforcer prudemment ses effectifs au cours des prochaines années, tant dans le domaine de l'urbanisme que de l'architecture. Il considère comme une chance d'avoir pu, en tant que conseiller,

Gegenüber der alt-neuen Häuserzeile am Markt soll der städtebauliche Vorschlag von cba zusammen mit Meurer Architekten der Kubatur der verlorenen mittelalterlichen Bebauung folgen und dennoch mit den Mitteln unserer Zeit zugleich Stadt reparieren und neu definieren.

Städtebau Vorsichtig wachsen soll sein Büro in den nächsten Jahren nach Wunsch von Christian Bauer – und zwar im Städtebau ebenso wie im klassischen Hochbau. Er betrachtet es als Glück, dass er als Be-

orthodox tenets of conventional modernism is currently experiencing a somewhat arduous second wave of urbanization. The objective is to turn the formerly mono-functional "dumping ground for office buildings" into a livable, fully-fledged part of the city of Luxembourg. As advisor to the "Fonds d'Urbanisation et d'Aménagement du Plateau de Kirchberg" Bauer personally came into contact with some of the most acclaimed architects of our time such as Richard Meier and Ricardo Bofill. Taking inspiration from such intellectually and artistically stimulating meetings, Christian Bauer

suivre au long cours la croissance rapide du projet de développement urbain le plus important du Luxembourg, et les problèmes qui y sont attachés. Nous voulons bien sûr parler du plateau de Kirchberg, le quartier phare de Luxembourg, qui regroupe en son sein presque toutes les institutions et les banques qui ont donné au pays, au cours des 40 dernières années, son rang sur la scène internationale et sa prospérité supérieure à la moyenne. Ce quartier, conçu à l'origine selon les canons du modernisme classique, traverse, péniblement, une deuxième vague d'urbanisation. Il s'agit de lui insuffler vie,

rater über viele Jahre hinweg das schnelle Wachstum und auch die damit einhergehenden Probleme von Luxemburgs wichtigstem neuen Stadtentwicklungsprojekt mitverfolgen konnte. Die Rede ist natürlich vom Kirchberg-Plateau, dem Luxemburger Vorzeigestadtteil, der fast alle Institutionen und Banken in seinen Grenzen vereint, die Luxemburg in den letzten vier Jahrzehnten internationale Bedeutung und überdurchschnittliches Vermögen verschafft haben. Dieser ursprünglich nach den orthodoxen Vorstellungen der klassischen Moderne konzipierte Stadtteil ist derzeit dabei, müh-

  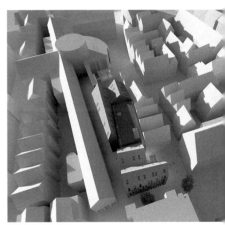

COMPETITION "JEWISH MUSEUM," COLOGNE (D), MENTION | COMPETITION "STADTHAUS AM MARKT," FRANKFURT AM MAIN (D), FOURTH PRIZE, INTERIOR VIEW AND URBAN SITUATION

and his team have created a strong profile for themselves in the field of large-scale projects over the last few years while their urban planning competition successes have opened up a promising new professional avenue. It is his wish that society and the political class take the built environment more seriously, and refrain from interpreting the act of building as a mere result of untamed market forces, putting faith back into the design process and enabling it to create a framework for the market to function in. In Luxembourg, a small country that

de transformer ce quartier, jadis monofonctionnel, simple collection de bâtiments de bureaux, en un quartier à vivre, à part entière. En tant que conseiller du Fonds d'Urbanisation et d'Aménagement du plateau de Kirchberg, Christian Bauer a longuement fréquenté quelques-uns des plus célèbres architectes contemporains, comme Richard Meier ou Ricardo Bofill. Nourris intellectuellement et artistiquement par ces rencontres, Christian Bauer et son cabinet ont, au cours de ces dernières années, acquis une solide compétence en matière de projets de

sam eine zweite Welle der Urbanisierung zu durchleben, die den einstigen monofunktionalen „Abwurfplatz für Bürobauten" zu einem lebenswerten, vollwertigen Stadtteil Luxemburgs machen soll. Als Berater des „Fonds d'Urbanisation et d'Aménagement du Plateau de Kirchberg" hat Bauer über viele Jahre hinweg persönlichen Kontakt mit einigen der namhaftesten Architekten unserer Zeit wie Richard Meier oder Ricardo Bofill gehabt. Von derlei intellektuell und künstlerisch inspirierenden Begegnungen ausgehend, haben Christian Bauer und sein Büro

has rapidly grown in the last few years, the negative effects of uncoordinated growth have been particularly painful. Architects have let themselves be carried away by the power of spectacular images. In many cases, images do nothing more than represent vacuous logos despite the fact that architecture, being a three-dimensional art form, can only properly unfold when a haptic and sensual spatial experience is created.

As advisor to the "Fonds d'Urbanisation et d'Aménagement du Plateau de Kirchberg," the institution, which was instrumental in developing one of the most exciting and controversial new towns in Europe, Christian Bauer was able to directly influence the urban development of New-Luxembourg. The urban regeneration that the famous plateau has been seeing for the last twenty years was designed to correct the deficiencies that resulted from modern urban planning following the CIAM (Congrès Internationaux d'Architecture Moderne) pattern. As planner and advisor, Bauer has for many years had a say in the transformation of the original plans and has been able to shape them to include a more pedestrian-friendly, urban vision. Frequently, this kind of urban regeneration proves to be more difficult than the planning of a new city from scratch. Bauer wants to replace drab traffic routes with high-quality urban space on the Kirchberg. Since planning culture was still rather underdeveloped in Luxembourg in the nineteen-sixties and -seventies, the regeneration of the Kirchberg plateau is a pioneer project whose significance is felt far beyond the country's borders.

While examining the theory and practice of the modernist city, Bauer has, in particular, been inspired by Jochem Jourdan from Frankfurt and the landscape architect Peter Latz from Bavaria. As leading personalities

grande envergure et, avec plusieurs succès enregistrés à des concours d'urbanisme, se sont engagés dans une nouvelle direction, prometteuse pour le cabinet.

Des politiques et de la société, Christian Bauer attend qu'ils prennent l'environnement construit plus au sérieux, qu'ils ne considèrent pas la construction comme le simple produit d'un marché débridé, mais qu'ils redonnent au contraire au projet son rôle, à savoir définir le cadre de ce marché. Au Luxembourg, petit pays qui a grandi d'un bond au cours des récentes décennies, on perçoit parfois de manière particulièrement douloureuse les inconvénients d'une croissance anarchique. Mais les architectes eux-mêmes sont aussi bien trop fascinés par le pouvoir qu'exercent des images spectaculaires ou séductrices. Bien trop souvent, les images se réduisent à des logos vides et plats, alors que l'architecture est un art en trois dimensions, dont l'intérêt réside justement dans la rencontre directe, sensible, haptique qu'il permet.

En tant que conseiller du Fonds d'Urbanisation et d'Aménagement du plateau de Kirchberg; l'institution qui a aidé à mettre au monde l'une des villes nouvelles les plus excitantes et les plus controversées d'Europe, Christian Bauer a été régulièrement en mesure d'exercer une influence directe sur le développement urbanistique de ce « Nouveau Luxembourg ». La transformation urbaine que connaît le célèbre plateau depuis maintenant environ 20 ans a toujours visé à corriger les défauts de l'urbanisme moderne selon le modèle du CIAM (Congrès Internationaux d'Architecture Moderne). Pendant de nombreuses années, Christian Bauer, à la fois comme auteur de projets et comme conseiller du Fonds, a influé sur la transformation du projet original, au bénéfice d'une vision plus urbaine, fai-

in den letzten Jahren ein starkes eigenes Profil beim Entwerfen im großen Maßstab gewonnen und mit mehreren städtebaulichen Wettbewerbserfolgen auch eine neue, zusätzliche und vielversprechende Richtung für das Büro eingeschlagen.

Von Politik und Gesellschaft wünscht sich Bauer, dass sie die gebaute Umwelt ernster nehmen und das Bauen nicht als bloßes Resultat eines ungezügelten Marktes interpretieren, sondern im Gegenteil dem Entwurf wieder die Kompetenz zukommen lassen, die Rahmen des Marktes vorzugeben. In Luxemburg, als kleinem und in den letzten Jahren sprunghaft gewachsenem Land, spürt man die Nachteile unkoordinierten Wachstums bisweilen besonders schmerzlich. Zu sehr ist aber auch der eigene Berufsstand der Architekten von der Macht spektakulärer oder verführerischer Bilder fasziniert, zu oft werden Bilder als leere Logos strapaziert, obwohl die Baukunst als dreidimensionale Kunstform ihren Reiz gerade in der unmittelbaren, sinnlich-haptischen Begegnung hat.

Als Berater des „Fonds d'Urbanisation et d'Aménagement du Plateau de Kirchberg", der Institution, die bei der Entstehung einer der aufregendsten und kontroversesten Neustädte in Europa beteiligt war, hat Christian Bauer immer wieder direkten Einfluss auf die städtebauliche Entwicklung Neu-Luxemburgs nehmen können. Der Stadtumbau, den das berühmte Plateau nun seit etwa 20 Jahren erlebt, war hier stets darauf gerichtet, die Defizite des modernen Städtebaus nach CIAM-Muster (Congrès Internationaux d'Architecture Moderne) zu revidieren. Als Planer und Berater hat Bauer an der Überformung der ursprünglichen Planung zugunsten einer fußgängerfreundlicheren, urbaneren Vision über viele Jahre hinweg Einfluss gehabt. Oft erwies sich dieser Stadtumbau als schwieriger als ein Stadt-Neubau. Bauer

in their fields, both have brought a new sense of scale, quality and radicality to Luxembourg which had been unknown in the country before.

Roots Following the completion of his studies at the ETH in Zurich, Bauer returned home to a completely changed country. At the time, Luxembourg was in transition, a booming and internationalizing country, which was also fast developing a new building culture. Bauer, however, was not blindly caught in the maelstrom of change. He had been influenced by the Swiss sociologist Lucius Burckhardt whom he had got to know in Switzerland as a student. It was Burckhardt's dictum that good architecture is not the result of an unquestioning implementation of a space allocation plan that left a deep impression on the young Bauer. This is because even if functions and uses change, the buildings that house them remain. Bauer wanted to create flexible spaces that would go beyond program specifications. He didn't want ground plans to be too function-specific to allow them to be used for other potential purposes over the span of many years.

Perhaps even more important than the sociological impulse was, however, the blossoming of the postmodern approach at the time. The American architecture theorist Robert Venturi and his plea for the rediscovery of symbolism in architecture, in opposition to the *tabula rasa* approach of modern planning, also deeply influenced Bauer. Venturi's ability to reconnect architecture with popular culture was unique.

Early Work Back in Luxembourg, Bauer first designed the Kornerup and Lygum Houses for sophisticated foreign clients who stood outside the Luxembourg context, just like

sant une plus juste place aux piétons. Une transformation urbaine souvent plus délicate que la construction d'une ville nouvelle, et pour laquelle Christian Bauer s'attache à substituer aux axes de circulation dépouillés de véritables espaces urbains. La culture urbanistique du Luxembourg des années 1960 et 70 était encore sous-développée et le modelage et le remodelage du plateau du Kirchberg constituent un projet pionnier dont la portée s'étend bien au-delà du Luxembourg, et qui est suivi au niveau international avec grand intérêt.

Christian Bauer, dans son approche de cette ville emblématique du modernisme, s'est surtout laissé inspirer par l'architecte Jochem Jourdan, de Francfort, et le paysagiste bavarois Peter Latz. Personnalités de premier plan dans leur domaine respectif, tous deux ont introduit de nouveaux standards, une nouvelle qualité et de la radicalité, auparavant inconnue au Luxembourg.

Racines Ses études à l'École polytechnique fédérale de Zurich achevées, Christian Bauer s'en était retourné au pays, un pays qu'il retrouvait métamorphosé. Le Luxembourg s'était éveillé ; on assistait au boom économique, à l'internationalisation, au développement rapide de l'architecture. Le jeune architecte se garda bien, pourtant, de se laisser happer par le tourbillon. Le sociologue suisse Lucius Burckhardt, que Bauer avait rencontré lorsqu'il était étudiant, avait en effet remis en question de manière trop radicale la mission de l'architecte qui se bornerait à construire des bâtiments. Bauer avait parfaitement intégré le précepte selon lequel l'application sans discernement d'un programme ne suffit pas à produire une bonne architecture. Car si les fonctions changent, les bâtiments, eux, demeurent. Bauer

will auf dem Kirchberg bloße Verkehrsstränge durch echte Stadträume ersetzen. Da die Planungskultur in den sechziger und siebziger Jahren in Luxemburg noch unterentwickelt war, ist die Formung und Überformung des Kirchberg-Plateaus ein Pionierprojekt, dessen Bedeutung weit über Luxemburg hinausgeht und international mit großem Interesse verfolgt wird.

Inspirieren lassen hat sich Bauer in seiner Auseinandersetzung mit der Stadt der Moderne speziell von Jochem Jourdan aus Frankfurt und dem Landschaftsarchitekten Peter Latz aus Bayern. Beide haben jeweils als führende Persönlichkeiten in ihrem Feld einen neuen Maßstab, eine neue Qualität und auch Radikalität nach Luxemburg gebracht, die zuvor unbekannt waren.

Wurzeln Nach dem Studium an der ETH in Zürich kehrte Bauer in seine Heimat zurück und fand sie völlig verändert vor. Luxemburg war damals ein Land im Aufbruch, das boomte und sich schnell internationalisierte und baukulturell entwickelte. Bauer stürzte sich jedoch nicht blind in den Sog. Der Schweizer Soziologe Lucius Burckhardt, dem er in der Schweiz als Student begegnet war, hatte den bloßen Auftrag des Architekten, Gebäude zu bauen, wohl zu gründlich hinterfragt. Das Diktum, dass das kritiklose Umsetzen eines Raumprogramms allein noch nicht zur guten Architektur führen kann, hat sich Bauer tief eingeprägt. Denn während Funktionen wechseln, sollen Gebäude bleiben. Bauer wollte Räume schaffen, die eine Nutzung erlauben, aber nicht allein von den Programmvorgaben abhängen. Die Grundrisse etwa sollten nicht zu nutzungsspezifisch sein, um auch nach vielen Jahren noch für andere Zwecke dienen zu können.

Noch wichtiger als der Impuls der Soziologie war jedoch die damals blühende Ästhetik

the houses in the end, too: they are unusually compact and open, with slanting roofs and double access routes. The Lygum House even has a brick façade, something that is rather unusual in Luxembourg.

Already in Bauer's early villa designs, such as the Fenigstein, Brouch or Biwer Houses, the architect's ecological sensibility is evident. With his concepts for solar water heating and the application of thermal buffers in his buildings, he has done pioneering work in Luxembourg. At the beginning of Christian Bauer's career, the issue of bioclimatic approaches in the design of detached

voulait créer des locaux adaptés à l'usage souhaité, mais sans dépendre exclusivement des contraintes du programme. Les plans, par exemple, ne devaient pas satisfaire trop spécifiquement un usage donné de manière à assurer la flexibilité nécessaire pour pouvoir encore servir bien des années plus tard, une fois les usages modifiés.

Plus encore que l'apport de la sociologie, ce sont l'esthétique et la mentalité postmodernistes de l'époque qui comptèrent pour Christian Bauer. Sa pensée se trouva durablement influencée, surtout, par le théoricien de l'architecture, l'américain Robert

und Geisteshaltung der Postmoderne. Vor allem der amerikanische Architekturtheoretiker Robert Venturi und sein Plädoyer für die Wiederentdeckung der Symbolik in der Architektur und die Opposition gegen die Tabula rasa des modernen Planens hatte Bauers Denken nachhaltig beeinflusst. In Venturis Vermögen, die Architektur zugleich wieder enger an die Populärkultur anzubinden, lag ein ungehobener Schatz.

Frühe Werke Zurück in Luxemburg, entwarf Bauer zunächst die Häuser Kornerup und Lygum für progressive ausländische Bau-

LYGUM HOUSE, NIEDERANVEN (L) | POOS HOUSE, SENNINGERBERG (L) | KORNERUP HOUSE, SENNINGERBERG (L)

houses was all-important. The Fenigstein House already had solar collectors for heating water.

At the time, this sort of work still resembled a pioneering research project that explored uncharted territory. Many concepts were still new, even among the majority of professional engineers. Simple principles were applied, such as those that have collectively become known under the label of "passive house" and that included the advantageous orientation of a building according to the points of the compass and the utilization of

Venturi, avec son plaidoyer pour la redécouverte de la symbolique dans l'architecture et son opposition à la pratique de la tabula rasa du modernisme. Dans la capacité de Robert Venturi à rapprocher à nouveau l'architecture de la culture populaire se trouvait une richesse à explorer.

L'œuvre précoce De retour au Luxembourg, Christian Bauer conçut d'abord les maisons Kornerup et Lygum. Ses commanditaires, des étrangers à l'avant-garde, étaient tout aussi extérieurs au microcosme luxembour-

herren, die ebenso außerhalb des luxemburgischen Kontextes standen wie die Häuser letztlich auch: Ungewöhnlich kompakt, mit Schrägdach und doppelter Erschließung entstanden offene Häuser, im Falle des Hauses Lygum sogar mit Backsteinfassade, was in Luxemburg besonders ungewöhnlich ist.

Schon bei den frühen eigenständigen Villenentwürfen von Bauer, wie für die Häuser Fenigstein, Brouch oder Biwer, zeigt sich auch die ökologische Sensibilität des Architekten, der mit seinen Konzepten zur solaren Warmwassergewinnung und dem Einsatz

atriums as thermal buffers. The design of the Biwer House had the objective of finding a sphere-like compact shape for the building that would reduce thermal loss to a minimum in winter. A Trombe wall functions like a narrow, naturally ventilated greenhouse that acts as a solar collector, rounding off the architecture of the house. On the other hand, the Brouch House has a more formal design that includes triple glazing and an internal, unheated winter garden, reducing energy costs.

These early villa designs exemplify Bauer's architectural influences as well as the devel-

geois que, en fin de compte, les maisons elles-mêmes : inhabituellement compactes, avec toit en pente et double accès, il s'agissait de maisons ouvertes, avec même une façade en briques pour la maison Lygum, ce qui est particulièrement inhabituel au Luxembourg.

Dès ses premiers projets autonomes de villas, comme les maisons Fenigstein, Brouch ou Biwer, la sensibilité écologique de l'architecte apparaît. C'est un véritable travail de pionnier qu'il effectue au Luxembourg dans ce domaine, avec ses concepts de production d'eau chaude solaire et l'utilisation d'es-

thermischer Puffer in seinen Gebäuden in Luxemburg regelrecht Pionierarbeit geleistet hat. Am Beginn der Karriere von Christian Bauer stand die Auseinandersetzung mit bioklimatischen Erwägungen im Einfamilienhausbau im Vordergrund. Schon beim Haus Fenigstein wurden Sonnenkollektoren zur Warmwassererzeugung eingesetzt und architektonisch thematisiert. Damals glich diese Arbeit noch einem Forschungsprojekt in unbekanntem Territorium, das Konzept war auch bei den Fachingenieuren noch größtenteils unbekannt. Einfache Prinzipien, wie sie heute unter dem Label „Passivhaus" be-

BIWER HOUSE, EHLANGE (L) | BROUCH HOUSE, LUXEMBOURG-CENTS (L) | FENIGSTEIN HOUSE, MOUTFORT (L)

opment of a personal approach: Bauer had studied the early work of Ricardo Bofill who had come to Luxembourg in the nineteen-nineties and had significantly influenced the urban development of the Kirchberg plateau. Another influence on Bauer was Charles Moore, especially his house in Sea Ranch, California, built in 1965, which exemplified the trend back to vernacular architecture and nature, as well as to a more popular morphology. Bauer did not, however, want to remain a villa-designing architect only. His intention was to bring the quality

paces tampons thermiques. Au début de sa carrière, sa prise en compte de considérations bioclimatiques concerne les maisons individuelles. Pour la maison Fenigstein déjà, il utilise des capteurs solaires pour la production d'eau chaude, qu'il intègre architecturalement. À l'époque, ce travail s'apparente au défrichage d'un terrain encore insuffisamment investi par les ingénieurs. Il applique aussi des principes simples, tels qu'on les connaît aujourd'hui sous l'appellation de « maison passive », comme l'orientation judicieuse du bâtiment et l'utilisation

kannt sind, wie die geschickte Orientierung des Gebäudes nach den Himmelsrichtungen und die Nutzung eines Atriums als thermischer Puffer, wurden hier bereits eingesetzt. Dem Entwurf für das Haus Biwer lag das Bestreben zugrunde, eine möglichst kugelähnliche, kompakte Form für das Gebäude zu finden, die den winterlichen Wärmeverlust auf ein Minimum verringert. Eine Wärmespeicherwand (*mur Trombe*) wirkt wie ein schmales, natürlich belüftetes Treibhaus, das als Sonnenkollektor die Form des Baus vervollständigt. Beim Haus Brouch hingegen,

of villa design to the design of apartments. This meant exploring acoustic decoupling, density, and the aesthetic atmosphere of spaces. At the time, however, models for high-quality multistory dwellings did not yet exist in Luxembourg. The first large offices and education facilities that were built, such as the Banque Indosuez or the Centre Universitaire already then met energy standards that have become commonplace only today. The Indosuez bank building, for instance, has box-type windows fitted in a particularly narrow façade that boasts of a heat recovery system to reduce heating

d'un atrium comme tampon thermique. Pour la maison Biwer, le projet s'était efforcé de trouver une forme compacte, aussi proche que possible de la sphère, afin de réduire au maximum les déperditions thermiques hivernales. Un mur Trombe, capteur solaire agissant à la manière d'une serre étroite, ventilée naturellement, complète la maison. Dans le cas de la maison Brouch, de conception plus formelle, les économies d'énergie sont obtenues par un triple vitrage et un jardin d'hiver intérieur non chauffé. Ces tout premiers projets de villas montrent Christian Bauer aux prises avec ses maî-

das formaler gestaltet ist, helfen eine Dreifachverglasung und ein interner, unbeheizter Wintergarten, Energiekosten zu sparen. Diese frühen Villenentwürfe zeigen die Auseinandersetzung mit Bauers Vorbildern ebenso wie die Entwicklung einer eigenständigen Haltung: Das Frühwerk von Ricardo Bofill, der später in den neunziger Jahren nach Luxemburg kam und entscheidenden Einfluss auf die städtebauliche Entwicklung des Kirchberg-Plateaus nahm, hatte Bauer studiert. Aber auch Charles Moore, speziell sein Haus in Sea-Ranch/Kalifornien von 1965 und die Tendenz zurück zur vernakulären Ar-

ADMINISTRATIVE BUILDING OF THE A&P KIEFFER OMINITEC COMPANY, LUXEMBOURG (L) | BANQUE INDOSUEZ, LUXEMBOURG (L), STREET VIEW AND ENTRANCE DETAIL

energy. It was in this building that, for the first time, ceilings were not suspended but designed as ribbed ceilings to activate the concrete used in them as thermal mass.

In more recent projects, such as the Kieffer office building, the range of applied bioclimatic measures was extended to include a sophisticated sun-shading system. The building for the Central Bank of Luxembourg, for instance, was equipped with a doubleglazed façade with movable sun-shading louvers made of glass.

The Centre Universitaire, Bauer's first large

tres, et l'émergence d'une posture personnelle. Bauer avait étudié l'œuvre précoce de Ricardo Bofill – qui vint plus tard, dans les années 90, à Luxembourg et exerça une influence déterminante sur l'aménagement urbain du plateau de Kirchberg. Charles Moore aussi influença Bauer, tout particulièrement ses maisons de Sea-Ranch (Californie, 1965), et sa tendance au retour à une architecture vernaculaire, à une forme populaire, à la nature. Christian Bauer ne souhaitait toutefois pas se cantonner à des villas, il aspirait plutôt à transposer les qualités de ce type

chitektur, zur populären Form und zur Natur hat Bauer beeinflusst. Er wollte aber kein reiner Villenarchitekt sein, sondern vielmehr die Qualitäten des Villenbaus auch in den Geschosswohnungsbau übertragen: Dazu gehören die akustische Entkoppelung, die Dichte und die raumgestalterische Qualität. In Luxemburg gab es damals jedoch noch kaum Modelle für qualitätvollen Geschosswohnungsbau.

Die ersten großen Büro- und Bildungsbauten wie die Banque Indosuez oder das Centre Universitaire folgen ebenfalls – erst

public assignment—though explicitly post-modern—avoided decorativeness.

Materials In Bauer's architecture practice, the choice of suitable building materials is determined by two factors: the context and ecology. Textured, tactile surfaces are preferred over neutral ones. Very often, nature becomes the model to which architects turn when they look for "decorative principles." A tangible materiality helps in avoiding a sense of undefined abstraction in a building design. Large concrete surfaces, for example, don't necessarily have to come across as clinical

d'habitations – le découplage acoustique, la compacité, la qualité de l'aménagement intérieur – aux immeubles d'habitation, à une époque où il n'existait pratiquement pas de modèles d'immeubles d'habitation de qualité au Luxembourg.

Les premières grandes constructions de bureaux ou d'établissements d'enseignement, comme la banque Indosuez ou le Centre universitaire, appliquaient également des principes énergétiques qui ne sont entrés qu'aujourd'hui dans les mœurs. Le bâtiment de la banque Indosuez est équipé par exemple de doubles fenêtres installées

heute gängigen – energetischen Prinzipien. Das Bankhaus der Indosuez beispielsweise hat Kastenfenster, die in einer besonders schmalen Fassade sitzen und über eine Wärmerückgewinnung dabei helfen, Heizenergie zu sparen. Bei diesem Gebäude wurden auch erstmals die Decken nicht abgehängt, sondern als Rippendecken architektonisch gestaltet, um die Betondecken als thermische Masse aktivierbar zu machen. Das Centre Universitaire, der erste große öffentliche Auftrag, war in der Haltung explizit postmodern, aber nicht dekorativ.

Bei den jüngeren Projekten wie dem Büro-

CENTRE UNIVERSITAIRE, SCIENCE WING, LUXEMBOURG (L) WITH PERRY WEBER UND RAYMOND THEISEN, ENTRANCE DETAIL AND OVERALL VIEW | MONTEREY BUILDING, CENTRAL BANK, LUXEMBOURG (L)

and distanced. Rough sawn wooden lagging or sandblasting can go a long way in giving them a more human feel.

Good Architecture Begins with Good Urban Planning The respectful approach towards historical buildings that is evident in Bauer's designs also shapes the architect's urban planning methodology: the preservation of historical buildings and of infrastructure not only brings ecological and economic advantages with it, but also serves to retain and reinforce specific identities of places.

dans une façade de faible épaisseur, qui permettent de récupérer la chaleur et d'économiser l'énergie de chauffage. Dans ce bâtiment, pour la première fois également, on supprimait les plafonds suspendus de manière à pouvoir utiliser l'inertie thermique du béton, et on optait pour un plancher à poutrelles et entrevous dont on soignait l'esthétique. La palette des solutions bioclimatiques a été judicieusement étendue à l'occasion de projets plus récents, comme l'immeuble de bureaux Kieffer, qui intègre un système de protection solaire sophistiqué, ou la Banque

haus Kieffer wurde die Palette der bioklimatischen Möglichkeiten um ein ausgeklügeltes Sonnenschutzsystem und beim Bau der Zentralbank von Luxemburg um eine doppelte Glasfassade mit ebenfalls gläsernen, beweglichen Sonnenschutzlamellen sinnvoll erweitert.

Materialien Die Wahl der geeigneten Baustoffe wird im Büro Bauer von zwei Merkmalen bestimmt: dem Kontext und der Ökologie. Taktile, haptische Oberflächen werden dabei neutralen stets vorgezogen.

During the new masterplanning of Dudelange in Luxembourg, for instance, the aim of the planners was to create urban density while maintaining large open spaces. In his endeavor to prefer the internal development of a city to its external shape, following the leitmotif of the "European City" with its consciously designed streets and squares, Rob Krier's theories on urban form have been a crucial influence. Public spaces ought to be prioritized over flashy free-standing buildings, while symbols of society need to come before the expression of individual interests. These days, social cohesion has

centrale du Luxembourg, avec une double façade en verre et des lames brise-soleil orientables, également en verre.

Le Centre universitaire, première grande commande publique du cabinet, était explicitement postmoderne dans la posture, mais non dans la décoration.

Les matériaux Chez cba, le choix des matériaux de construction appropriés se fait selon deux critères : le contexte et l'écologie. Les surfaces tactiles, haptiques, sont toujours préférées aux surfaces neutres. Le modèle des « principes décoratifs » ser-

Dabei dient die Natur den Architekten oft als Vorbild für „dekorative Prinzipien", eine spürbare Materialität hilft die Abstraktion eines Gebäudeentwurfs aufzuheben. Große Betonoberflächen beispielsweise müssen nicht klinisch wirken, sondern können durch eine sägeraue Schalung oder Sandstrahlung eine menschlichere Dimension bekommen.

Gute Architektur beginnt im guten Städtebau Der Respekt dem Bestand gegenüber, der sich in Bauers Gebäuden zeigt, prägt auch seine städtebauliche Herange-

FACTORY SHED FOR ROTAREX, ECHTERNACH (L) | SENOIR CITIZEN'S RESIDENCE STRASSEN (L) | EUROPEAN SCHOOL, LUXEMBOURG (L) | MOKO VILLA, SCHUTTRANGE (L)

become rather weak and urban morphology reflects this problem all too clearly. For Bauer, providing new streets and squares is therefore not enough. He wants to holistically design them, taking into account their surface textures, their potential as meeting places or as street furniture. In order to underline residents' physical contact to the ground and the soil, Bauer prefers narrow townhouses that relate to the outside, wherever possible.

Lively cities, however, only emerge when uses are no longer strictly segregated,

vant à compenser l'abstraction d'un projet par une matérialité tangible, les architectes de cba l'ont trouvé dans la nature. Ainsi, le caractère froid et stérile des grandes surfaces en béton, par exemple, n'est pas une fatalité, l'emploi de coffrages en planches brutes de sciage ou le sablage pouvant leur conférer plus de mordant.

Un urbanisme de qualité pour une architecture de qualité Le respect de l'existant, qui apparaît dans les constructions de Bauer, marque aussi son approche urbanistique :

hensweise: Der Erhalt von Bestandsgebäuden und Infrastruktur ist schließlich nicht nur ökologisch und ökonomisch sinnvoll, er hilft auch dabei, die Identität eines Ortes zu bewahren und zu stärken. Beim städtebaulichen Plan für Dudelange in Luxemburg beispielsweise war es das Ziel der Entwerfer, städtische Dichte zu schaffen und dennoch großzügige Freiräume zu erhalten. Im Bestreben, der Außen- die Innenentwicklung einer Stadt stets vorzuziehen und dem Leitbild der „europäischen Stadt" mit ihren bewusst gestalteten Straßen und Plätzen

when living, working, and recreation happen in one and the same place and journey distances are short. When places of work are mostly located in anonymous industrial or commercial zones at the edge of a city, it loses a crucial dimension. Industrial arts and artisanry, at least, ought to be brought back to the shop windows as Bauer pleads for in his urban planning concepts, in order that customer ties are strengthened and the relocation of work places to vacuous urban peripheries is reduced.

For Bauer, economic thinking is inextricably linked to urban planning and should not be

tout bien considéré, la conservation des bâtiments et de l'infrastructure existants n'est pas seulement pertinente du point de vue écologique et économique, elle sert aussi, dans ce cas, à maintenir et à renforcer l'identité d'un lieu. Pour le plan d'urbanisme de la ville de Dudelange, au Luxembourg, l'objectif du cabinet a été, par exemple, de parvenir à une densité urbaine satisfaisante tout en maintenant des espaces libres généreux. L'influence des travaux théoriques de Rob Krier sur l'urbanisme apparaît, aujourd'hui encore, dans les projets de Christian Bauer et dans sa préférence résolue à la fois pour

gerecht zu werden, zeigt sich bis heute in Bauers Entwürfen der Einfluss von Rob Kriers theoretischem Werk zum Städtebau. Öffentliche Räume sollten gegenüber Aufmerksamkeit heischenden Einzelgebäuden die Priorität genießen und die Symbole der Gesellschaft vor dem Ausdruck der Individualinteressen stehen. Heute ist der gesellschaftliche Zusammenhang oft nur schwach ausgeprägt und der Städtebau reflektiert dieses Problem leider oft überdeutlich. Die Schaffung von Straßen und Plätzen alleine genügt Bauer deshalb nicht, er will sie auch gestalten – als Oberfläche, als Aufenthalts-

NATIONAL MUSEUM OF HISTORY AND ART, LUXEMBOURG (L), PREHISTORIC SECTION AND ATRIUM ROOM ABOVE | BAUER-RAFFAELLI HOUSE, LUXEMBOURG (L) | EUROPEAN SCHOOL, LUXEMBOURG (L)

neglected, especially in cases where social concerns are to be addressed within a framework dominated by private companies and investors.

Bauer's abstract urban planning goals depend on the size of the city: in smaller cities he prefers a clear demarcation of limits between the cities and their surrounding landscapes, i.e., between human creation and open nature. When cities grow to a certain larger size, however, he feels that planners ought to bring landscape elements into these dense cities. This can take the form of

le développement intérieur d'une ville plutôt que son expansion aux marges et pour le modèle de la « ville européenne », avec ses rues et ses places dont l'aménagement procède d'une intention forte. Les espaces publics doivent l'emporter sur l'individualité de bâtiments qui forceraient l'attention, de même que les symboles de ce qui fait la société doivent l'emporter sur l'expression des égoïsmes. Aujourd'hui, le lien social est souvent faible et cet état de fait est souvent aussi, hélas, reflété à outrance par l'urbanisme. Créer des rues et des places ne suffit

ort oder als Stadtmöbel. Um den physischen Kontakt aller Bewohner eines Ortes mit dem Erdboden zu stärken, bevorzugt Bauer – wo es angebracht ist – schmale Stadthäuser mit Bezug zum Außenraum.

Lebendige Städte entstehen aber erst, wenn die Nutzungen nicht länger streng getrennt werden, wenn Leben, Arbeiten und Erholen an ein und demselben Ort stattfinden können und die Wege dementsprechend kurz sind. Wenn die Arbeitsplätze mehrheitlich in anonymen Gewerbegebieten am Rande der Stadt angesiedelt sind, geht der Stadt eine

"pocket parks" or of a "green mesh," according to Bauer. As dust-binding agent and carbon dioxide absorber, providing coolness and moisture, vegetation has a crucial role to play in making cities livable, both in a social and an aesthetic sense. It is also essential in ecologic and climatic terms. As Le Corbusier had suggested, roof surfaces can even be used for playing tennis or growing tomatoes in the city, turning them into mini-parks, as it were.

The Team Is the Star The office of cba is headed by Christian Bauer and four other partners whose strength lies in their complementary skills. The firm's rapid growth has proved to be an advantage since a larger size is a prerequisite for the successful handling of certain project types. Design competitions represent the most preferred type of project acquisition, particularly abroad. A competitive spirit and the encounter with the European elite have made the firm strong. The office is also understandably proud of its direct project appointments owing to its excellent references. Then there are project partnerships and collaborations with international partners that offer the op-

par conséquent pas à Christian Bauer, il veut aussi les rendre « habitables », en aménageant des lieux de repos, en soignant les surfaces, en choisissant le mobilier urbain. Pour renforcer le contact physique des habitants avec la terre, Bauer préfère – là où cela est opportun – d'étroites maisons de ville, reliées à l'extérieur.

Les villes ne deviennent toutefois vivantes que si les usages ne sont plus séparés de manière stricte, si l'on peut vivre, travailler, se reposer en un même lieu et si les distances à parcourir sont réduites à un minimum. Lorsque les emplois sont majoritairement implantés dans des zones d'activité anonymes, aux confins de la ville, celle-ci perd une de ses dimensions essentielles. Dans ses projets d'urbanisme, Christian Bauer encourage à « rapprocher au moins les activités artisanales des vitrines », et donc de la clientèle, ce qui limite aussi le rejet des emplois vers la périphérie.

Pour Bauer, la pensée économique est indissociable du projet urbanistique si l'on veut que la primauté de l'initiative économique privée puisse être encadrée par une société forte.

ganz entscheidende Dimension verloren. Bauer regt in seinen städtebaulichen Planungen an, dass zumindest handwerkliche Produktion wieder „bis an das Schaufenster herangeführt werden kann", um die Kundenbindung zu erhöhen und das Abschieben der Arbeitsplätze auf die grüne Wiese an der Peripherie zu mildern.

Für Bauer gehört wirtschaftliches Denken untrennbar zum städtebaulichen Entwurf; gerade wenn die Dominanz der Initiative durch private Unternehmer durch ein starkes Engagement der Gesellschaft ergänzt werden soll, ist es unerlässlich, die ökonomischen Gesichtspunkte nicht aus dem Blick zu verlieren.

Bauers abstrakte Ziele im Städtebau hängen von der Größe der Stadt ab: Bei kleineren Städten bevorzugt er die klare Zäsur zwischen Stadt und Landschaft, zwischen dem menschlichen Werk und der offenen Natur. Wenn Städte jedoch eine bestimmte Größe überschreiten, sollte es Aufgabe der Planer sein, Landschaftselemente auch in die dicht bebaute Stadt zu bringen – und zwar sowohl in Form von klar konturierten *Pocket Parks* als auch als „grünes Gewebe". Als Staub-

WATER STRIP PROJECT, TRIER (D) | GREEN HILL HOUSING PROJECT, LUXEMBOURG (L), OVERALL VIEW

portunity to diversify into new building typologies and scales.

Christian Bauer and his partners are anything but "lonesome wolves." Constant dialog with each other is a basic need for them, something that helps motivate them to maintain a high project standard. They are not content with just producing good designs. They want to excel in implementing them, too. Quite consciously, the firm does not have a specific aesthetic style it sticks to because it believes that the shape of a building cannot be arbitrarily predetermined but emerges from the requirements

Les objectifs que, dans l'absolu, Christian Bauer fixe à l'urbanisme varient selon la taille de la ville : dans le cas de villes de taille modeste, il préfère la césure claire entre la ville et la campagne environnante, entre l'œuvre humaine « minérale » et la nature. Mais lorsque les villes dépassent une certaine taille, il revient aux urbanistes d'introduire des éléments du paysage à l'intérieur de la ville dense – et ce, à la fois sous forme de petits espaces verts, « parcs de poche » aux contours bien définis, et de « trames vertes ». La végétation fixe les poussières et absorbe le CO_2, elle dispense fraîcheur

binder und CO_2-Absorber, dabei Kühle und Feuchte spendend, hilft Vegetation bei der Gestaltung lebenswerter Städte – in sozialer wie ästhetischer Hinsicht. Ihr kommen zudem handfeste ökologische und klimatische Aufgaben zu. Wie schon Le Corbusier vorschlug, könnten selbst Dachflächen fürs Tennisspielen und Tomatenzüchten in der Stadt herangezogen werden und zu kleinen Miniparks werden.

Das Team ist der Star Das Büro cba wird von Christian Bauer und vier weiteren Partnern geführt, deren Stärke in ihren kom-

GREEN HILL HOUSING PROJECT, LUXEMBOURG (L), STREETVIEW | MASTER PLAN DUDELANGE SCHMELZ, DUDELANGE (L)

of a place and the nature of the task at hand. It is a product of the designer's ideas and not a fixed starting point in itself. If we were to look for adjectives that describe the works of cba we would have to say that they are consistent, of a high standard, rigorous and coherent yet lucid. The firm's focus lies on specific project ideas and not on a universally applicable architectural vocabulary.

Prospects for the Future In the coming years, cba intends to complete a range of

et humidité : elle a non seulement un rôle social et esthétique dans l'aménagement de villes à vivre, elle remplit aussi un sérieux rôle écologique et climatique. Comme Le Corbusier le prévoyait déjà, les toitures pourraient même devenir des miniparcs et être utilisées pour jouer au tennis ou faire pousser des tomates en pleine ville.

L'équipe tient la vedette Le cabinet cba est dirigé par Christian Bauer et quatre autres partenaires dont la force repose sur la complémentarité des talents. La crois-

plementären Talenten begründet liegt. Das Wachstum, das das Büro erlebt hat, hat sich als Vorteil erwiesen, weil erst eine gewisse Größe die erfolgreiche Bearbeitung bestimmter Projektarten erlaubt. Wettbewerbe sind für cba die edelste Form der Akquise, besonders im Ausland. Das Reiben an der Konkurrenz und Messen mit der europäischen Elite hat das Büro stark gemacht. Aber auch auf einige Direktaufträge durch eigene Referenzen sind die Büroinhaber zu Recht stolz. Hinzu kommen Projektpartnerschaften und das Zusammenarbeiten mit

diverse projects: from the large new building for the University of Luxembourg at Esch-sur-Alzette, in collaboration with Baumschlager Eberle, to a large residential project at the water strip in Trier, to the elaborate IT data store Luxconnect in Bissen. For the last-mentioned project, the objective is to create a "house of servers" with a human touch. Its metallic façade was inspired by the Faraday cages in which the servers for data warehousing purposes will be located, giving it a homogeneous look and carefully hiding the elaborate technical facilities behind. The high-grade steel skin will generate a "clear and clean, universal image" for this free-standing building that is devoid of a context and that will resemble a "body swimming in the landscape."

Entirely different strategies were required for the water strip project in Trier to create a lively urban as well as economically healthy district. Located on a site that formerly housed the regional garden festivals, the building adroitly makes use of the topography to combine different urban facilities: a long bar-like block housing freehold apartments of different sizes rests on a series of four diversely designed boxes that offer commercial and service facilities. Some of the apartments are of the duplex type, allowing for a great deal of spatial flexibility.

Along with the increased internationalization of the office will come a stronger focus on urban planning projects. Even if urban planning is not considered to be an end in itself by the office, it does constitute the most important basis for all building designs.

sance des effectifs du cabinet s'est avérée un atout, une taille critique étant nécessaire pour mener à bien certains types de projets. Les concours constituent pour cba la forme la plus noble de prospection, en particulier à l'étranger ; à se frotter à la concurrence et à se mesurer à l'élite européenne, le cabinet s'est affirmé. Mais les associés sont également fiers, à juste titre, de certaines commandes directes, fruit de leurs propres références. À cela s'ajoutent des partenariats sur certains projets et des collaborations internationales, qui ouvrent parfois à de nouveaux types de bâtiments ou de nouvelles échelles d'intervention.

Christian Bauer et ses partenaires ne sont pas des « loups solitaires », ils ont besoin d'échanger sans cesse, pour s'aiguillonner mutuellement et maintenir les projets, et au-delà, les réalisations elles-mêmes, à un niveau élevé de qualité. Il n'y a pas, délibérément, de « style cba » que l'on identifierait à coup sûr : la forme des bâtiments ne relève pas du dogme, elle naît, à chaque fois nouvelle, des exigences du lieu et de la finalité du projet. Elle est le produit, et non le point de départ, de la réflexion des concepteurs. Détermination, qualité, rigueur, cohérence et clarté – telles sont les caractéristiques de chacune des réalisations de cba, et à chaque fois, c'est le concept propre au projet qui est au premier plan, non une écriture architectonique uniforme.

Perspectives Les années à venir verront la poursuite ou l'achèvement de projets très différents les uns des autres, qu'il s'agisse

internationalen Partnern, die bisweilen die Möglichkeit der Bearbeitung von neuen Bautypologien oder Maßstäben eröffnen. Christian Bauer und seine Partner sind keine „einsamen Wölfe", sie brauchen den ständigen Austausch untereinander, um sich gegenseitig anzuspornen und die Projekte auf hohem Niveau zu halten. Gut im Entwurf zu sein, genügt ihnen nicht, sie wollen auch gut in der Umsetzung sein. Dabei gibt es bewusst keinen unverkennbaren Stil des Büros, denn die Form der Gebäude ist keine Setzung, sondern entsteht stets neu aus den Anforderungen des Ortes und der Aufgabe heraus. Sie ist ein Produkt der Überlegungen der Entwerfer und nicht der Ausgangspunkt. Konsequent, qualitätvoll, streng, kohärent und verständlich – das sind die Adjektive, die jedes Werk von cba beschreiben. Im Vordergrund steht dabei jedoch stets die spezifische Projektidee und nicht eine einheitliche architektonische Handschrift.

Ausblick In den nächsten Jahren wird das Büro cba ganz unterschiedliche Projekte fertigstellen und weiter bearbeiten: vom großen Neubau für die Universität von Luxemburg in Esch-sur-Alzette, zusammen mit Baumschlager Eberle, über ein großes Wohnungsbauprojekt am Wasserband in Trier bis zur hochgezüchteten Behausung von IT-Technik wie bei dem Datenspeicher Luxconnect in Bissen. Bei diesem Projekt ging es darum, ein „Haus für Server" zu entwickeln, das dennoch menschlichen Ansprüchen genügt. Die Faraday'schen Käfige, in denen die Server für das Data-Warehousing stehen

des nouveaux bâtiments de l'université du Luxembourg à Esch-sur-Alzette – un grand projet en collaboration avec le cabinet Baumschlager Eberle –, d'un important projet de logements, « am Wasserband » à Trèves, ou encore de l'hébergement high-tech de systèmes informatiques comme avec le centre de données Luxconnect à Bissen. Avec ce projet, il s'agissait de proposer une « maison » pour des serveurs qui soit aussi une « maison » pour les opérateurs. Les cages de Faraday dans lesquelles seront placés les serveurs ont inspiré la façade métallique, gage d'homogénéité pour un volume simple, derrière laquelle les installations techniques coûteuses peuvent aisément être cachées. La peau en acier inoxydable garantira une « image claire et nette, parfaitement uniforme » pour ce bâtiment hors contexte, « flottant dans le paysage ».

Des stratégies tout autres furent nécessaires pour le projet « am Wasserband » à Trèves. Il s'agissait là de créer un quartier économiquement dynamique dans un urbanisme vivant. Sur l'ancien terrain qui avait accueilli les floralies de Rhénanie-Palatinat, les constructions utilisent habilement la topographie pour combiner entre eux différents usages urbains : une longue bande de logements en copropriété repose sur quatre parallélépipèdes tous différents, destinés aux commerces et aux services. Les logements, certains sous forme de duplex, sont de tailles variées et permettent des formes d'habitation totalement différenciées, en plan comme en élévation.

werden, boten die Inspiration für die metallische Fassade, die der einfachen Box ein homogenes Fassadenbild gibt, hinter dem auch spielend die aufwendigen technischen Installationen kaschiert werden können. Die Edelstahlhaut wird ein „klares, rundum einheitliches sauberes Bild" für diesen kontextlosen Solitärbau bilden, wie ein „schwimmender Körper in der Landschaft".

Ganz andere Strategien waren bei dem Projekt für das Wasserband in Trier nötig, um einen urbanistisch lebendigen und auch wirtschaftlich vitalen Stadtteil zu schaffen. Auf dem ehemaligen Gelände der Landesgartenschau nutzt der Bau die Topografie geschickt aus, um verschiedene städtische Nutzungen miteinander zu kombinieren: Über vier unterschiedlich gestalteten Boxen für Gewerbe und Dienstleistungen ruht ein langer Riegel mit Eigentumswohnungen unterschiedlicher Größe, die, teils als Maisonetten organisiert, im Grund- und Aufriss ganz verschiedene Wohnformen erlauben.

Neben der angestrebten zunehmenden Internationalisierung wird eine stärkere Gewichtung des städtebaulichen Entwerfens die Arbeit des Büros prägen. Denn auch, wenn der Städtebau nicht als Selbstzweck begriffen wird, bildet er doch die wichtigste Grundlage für alle Hochbauentwürfe.

PROJECTS

NATIONAL MUSEUM OF HISTORY AND ART, LUXEMBOURG (L)

MUSÉE NATIONAL D'HISTOIRE ET D'ART, LUXEMBOURG (L)
MUSÉE NATIONAL D'HISTOIRE ET D'ART, LUXEMBURG (L)

The sharply cut, natural stone cube of the National Museum of History and Art in the old part of Luxembourg is sharp in a figurative sense too: its entrance façade is almost entirely clad in a crisp and light limestone. Only a vertical strip of light and the entrance seem as if they have been cut out with a knife.

In 1997, the "Fonds de rénovation de la Vieille Ville" launched an architecture design competition for the renovation and construction of a new building for the museum. The objective was to more than double the existing exhibition space. Together, the new and the old building now house over 4,600 square meters of exhibition space. The new building, which seems large compared to the small scale of the old city, required a sensitive approach to its spatial arrangement.

The architecture of the museum creates a sense of suspense between the old and the new and an interesting interplay of gaps and interstitial spaces between the two domains. The spine of the museum is the existing historical townhouse. Between it and the new building a glass-covered crossing with ramps and bridges has been constructed, connecting the old and the new building.

Approaching visitors first leave the steep street, the Rue Sigefroi, and climb a few

Revêtu d'un calcaire clair, le Musée national d'histoire et d'art, dans la vieille ville de Luxembourg, se présente tel un imposant bloc de pierre anguleux. Seuls un étroit jour vertical et l'entrée entaillent sa façade principale.

En 1997, le « Fonds de rénovation de la Vieille Ville » avait lancé un concours d'architecture pour la restructuration du musée et la construction d'un nouveau bâtiment. Il s'agissait de doubler, voire plus, les surfaces d'exposition existantes : au total, la partie ancienne et la partie neuve abritent désormais plus de 4600 mètres carrés de surfaces d'exposition. Un chiffre important au regard de l'échelle réduite de la vieille ville, qui a exigé un réglage fin de l'organisation des espaces.

La tension entre neuf et ancien donne toute sa force au musée. Entre ces deux « mondes », l'architecture a introduit des articulations et des espaces de transition intéressants. Un élément abritant rampes et passerelles, couvert d'une verrière, fait « charnière » entre le nouveau bâtiment et l'ancienne maison bourgeoise, cœur historique de l'institution.

Pour accéder au musée, le visiteur doit gravir quelques marches depuis la rue Sigefroi, en pente, pour atteindre l'ancienne place du Marché aux Poissons, une des rares places

Der scharf geschnittene Natursteinquader des Museums für Geschichte und Kunst in der Altstadt von Luxemburg eckt im wahrsten Sinne des Wortes an: Seine Eingangsseite ist fast vollständig mit einem hellen Kalkstein verkleidet. Nur ein vertikales Lichtband und der Eingang sind wie mit dem Messer ausgeschnitten.

Der „Fonds de rénovation de la Vieille Ville" hatte 1997 einen Architekturwettbewerb für den Um- und Neubau des Museums ausgelobt. Die Ausstellungsfläche im bestehenden Altbau sollte dabei mehr als verdoppelt werden. Zusammen beherbergen Alt- und Neubau nun über 4600 Quadratmeter Ausstellungsfläche. Dieses für den kleinen Maßstab der Altstadt große Volumen forderte eine feine Gliederung.

Die Architektur des Museums lebt von der Spannung zwischen Alt und Neu und artikuliert interessante Fugen und Zwischenräume zwischen beiden Sphären. Das Rückgrat des Museums bildet das bestehende historische Bürgerhaus. Zwischen ihm und dem Neubau liegt ein glasüberdachtes Gelenk mit Rampen und Brücken, die Alt- und Neubau miteinander verknüpfen.

Wer das Museum besucht, steigt vom abschüssigen Straßenniveau der Rue Sigefroi zuerst ein paar Stufen hinauf auf die Ebene des Platzes, den ehemaligen Fischmarkt,

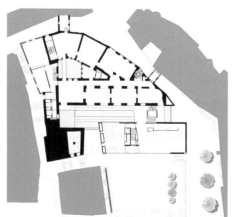
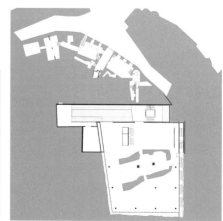

steps to the level of the square, the former fish market, one of the few remaining squares in the densely built-up old city. The foyer exudes an atmosphere of elegant restraint in terms of its morphology and materials. From there, visitors reach the large atrium whose ramps invite visitors to a "promenade architecturale," taking them five floors down to exhibits that display prehistory and early history. Visitors then leave behind the darkness of the early period and ascend to the light of modern times. Each section can, however, also be directly accessed.

The upper basement also houses a cellar vault dating from 1580 which has been chiseled into the sandstone rock. The rock foundation on which Luxembourg and the museum are built thus becomes the enduring aesthetic motif of the building.

The lighting concept elegantly amalgamates natural and artificial lighting. The lit up narrow gap on the front side forms the edge of the façade and takes up the line of the light strip at the end of the square. At the same time, this glass-clad gap admits daylight onto the lowermost level.

The contemporary architecture of the museum sensitively engages the existing historical building. The interplay between the old and the new makes for sensual visitor experiences, with strong color and material contrasts. Windows in the historical building provide views onto the courtyard. The restored historical façade of the old museum now finds itself inside.

The collection is displayed in a series of introverted cabinets, small and large rooms. All halls in which art is displayed have lit up ceilings. Together with the pastel-colored walls and the warm tone of the parquet floor they create a solemn atmosphere.

de ce cœur historique dense. Une impression d'élégance et de retenue se dégagent des formes et matières employées dans le hall. De celui-ci, on atteint le grand atrium dont les rampes invitent à une « promenade architecturale » vers le haut, du cinquième et dernier niveau de sous-sol, des profondeurs souterraines de la pré- et de la protohistoire. De là, on remonte en quelque sorte des ténèbres des premiers temps à la lumière des Temps modernes. Chaque section est également accessible directement si on le souhaite.

Le premier sous-sol comporte une voûte qui fut taillée dans le grès en 1580. La roche, sur laquelle est construite la Ville de Luxembourg et donc aussi le musée, constitue un motif que l'on retrouve ici partout.

Pour ce qui est de l'éclairage, l'architecture fait se fondre élégamment lumière artificielle et lumière naturelle. Ainsi, par exemple, l'étroit jour de la façade principale, à l'angle, est dans le prolongement du bandeau lumineux qui borde la place. Par ce jour vitré, la lumière naturelle pénètre jusqu'au dernier niveau de sous-sol.

L'architecture contemporaine du musée aborde avec sensibilité le bâtiment historique existant. Les transitions entre neuf et ancien, les contrastes forts dans les couleurs et les matériaux, mettent les sens en émoi. Par les fenêtres sur cour, on voit ce qui se passe dans le bâtiment historique dont la façade restaurée se trouve maintenant côté intérieur.

Les collections sont présentées dans une suite de cabinets secrets, de petites salles et de grands espaces. Toutes les salles dans lesquelles des œuvres d'art sont exposées, possèdent un plafond lumineux. L'éclairage doux, les tons pastel des murs et le ton chaud des parquets contribuent à créer une atmosphère de recueillement.

einen der wenigen Plätze in der dicht bebauten Altstadt. Das Foyer strahlt eine vornehme Zurückhaltung in Form und Material aus. Von dort gelangt man in das große Atrium, dessen Rampen zu einer „promenade architecturale" einladen – bis zu fünf Etagen in die unterirdischen Tiefen der Vor- und Frühgeschichte. Von dort steigt man gleichsam aus dem tiefen Dunkel der Frühzeit dem Licht der Neuzeit oder Moderne entgegen. Jede Abteilung kann aber auch direkt angesteuert werden.

Im ersten Untergeschoss wurde ein in den Sandsteinfelsen gehauenes Kellergewölbe von 1580 integriert. Der Fels, auf dem Luxemburg gebaut ist und auf dem auch das Museum gründet, wird zum durchgängigen Motiv des Hauses.

Die Lichtführung verquickt Natur- und Kunstlicht auf elegante Art. Die schmale Lichtspalte an der Schauseite bildet die Fassadenkante und nimmt die Linie des Lichtbands an der Platzbegrenzung auf. Gleichzeitig lässt diese Glasspalte Tageslicht bis in die unterste Ebene.

Die zeitgenössische Architektur des Museums geht sensibel auf den historischen Gebäudebestand ein. Durch die Übergänge zwischen Alt und Neu wird das Museum zu einem sinnlichen Erlebnisraum mit starken Kontrasten in Farben und Materialien. Durch die Fenster zum Hof blickt man im Altbau auf das Geschehen. Die restaurierte historische Fassade des alten Museums befindet sich nun im Innenraum.

Präsentiert wird die Sammlung in einer Folge aus introvertierten Kabinetten, kleineren und großen Räumen. Alle Säle, in denen Kunst ausgestellt ist, haben Lichtdecken. Sie sorgen im Zusammenklang mit den Pastelltönen der Wände und dem warmen Holzton der Parkettböden für eine andächtige Stimmung.

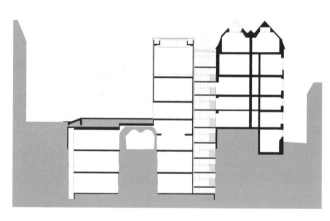

FORUM AT THE CATHEDRAL AND DIOCESAN MUSEUM, OSNABRÜCK (D)

FORUM DE LA CATHÉDRALE ET MUSÉE DIOCÉSAIN, OSNABRÜCK (D)
FORUM AM DOM UND DIÖZESANMUSEUM, OSNABRÜCK (D)

For around 1,200 years now, Osnabrück Cathedral and its surrounding buildings have continuously been renovated and extended. As such, the most recent conversion and addition, the redesign of the Diocesan Museum along with a choir hall and a pastoral care section stands in a long tradition extending over many centuries. The ensemble's long history demands respect but ought not to lead to the suppression of contemporary architectural vocabularies, and the resort to a historicist style instead. These ideas formed the foundation of the design of christian bauer & associés architectes, which was submitted in 2003 to an architectural design competition that involved ten firms. The architects were given the assignment to undertake the conversion and extension work together with the architects from Planungsbüro Rohling (pbr).

The task at the "Forum at the Cathedral" involved the construction of a newly designed information and reception area with a new entrance, as well as the renovation of the pastoral care spaces, a new rehearsal hall for choirs, and the cathedral museum. The cathedral treasury and diocesan museum, in particular, became areas of focus as they house unique treasures that deserve to be presented to the public in an attractive and

Depuis 1200 ans environ, la cathédrale d'Osnabrück et les constructions qui l'entourent ne cessent de faire l'objet de transformations et d'extensions. Les plus récentes, l'aménagement du Musée diocésain, d'une salle pour les répétitions des chorales et d'un espace d'accueil spirituel, s'inscrivent ainsi dans une extraordinaire continuité temporelle qui s'étend sur plusieurs siècles. Cette longue histoire exige le respect, mais ne doit pas être prétexte à réprimer un langage architectural contemporain au profit d'une architecture historiciste. C'est dans cet esprit que le cabinet cba a élaboré le projet présenté en 2003 dans le cadre d'un concours sur invitation qui alignait dix candidats. Cba, qui a remporté le concours et obtenu la commande des travaux de transformation et d'extension, s'est alors associé au bureau d'études Rohling (pbr).

L'opération portait non seulement sur l'aménagement d'un nouvel espace d'information et de rencontre, avec une nouvelle entrée, mais aussi sur la rénovation des espaces d'accueil spirituel, la construction d'une nouvelle salle de répétition pour les chorales et l'aménagement du musée de la cathédrale. Le Trésor et le Musée diocésain recèlent en effet des richesses qui méritent d'être présentées au public et exposées de manière

Der Dom von Osnabrück und die ihn umgebenden Bauten werden seit etwa 1200 Jahren immer wieder umgebaut und erweitert. Die jüngsten Um- und Anbauten, die Neugestaltung des Diözesanmuseums, des Chorsaals und des Seelsorgebereichs des Doms stehen also in einer atemberaubenden zeitlichen Kontinuität über viele Jahrhunderte. Die lange Geschichte verlangt Respekt, sollte aber nicht dazu verleiten, zeitgenössische Architektursprache zu unterdrücken und historisierend zu bauen. Dies war die Grundlage des Entwurfs von christian bauer & associés architectes, der im Rahmen eines geladenen Wettbewerbs mit zehn Büros 2003 eingereicht wurde. Die Architekten bekamen zusammen mit dem Planungsbüro Rohling (pbr) den Auftrag, die Um- und Erweiterungsarbeiten vorzunehmen.

Zu der Bauaufgabe „Forum am Dom" gehörten nicht nur ein neu gestalteter Informations- und Begegnungsbereich mit neuem Eingang, sondern auch die Renovierung der Räume der Seelsorge, ein neuer Probensaal für Chöre und das Dom-Museum. Besonders die Domschatzkammer und das Diözesanmuseum bergen Schätze, die es verdienen, in einer attraktiven, modernen Ausstellungsgestaltung der Öffentlichkeit präsentiert zu werden. Die mit bodentiefen

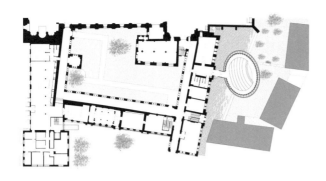

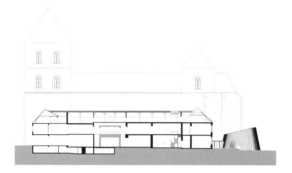

modern exhibition setting. The windows in the façade were extended to the floor. This spacious glazing along with the new entrance gate is opening the church to the urban space and makes its appearance more welcoming and appropriate.

Following the renovation, the cathedral museum resembles a series of cabinet-like linear spaces. Nine rooms in the southern wing of the cloister are today being used for a permanent exhibition while an additional room was provided for special exhibitions. Central to the museum is the former St. Margaret's Chapel in the cloister whose suspended ceiling, which was built in after the Second World War, was removed in order to make the space appear larger and more active. Resting on four stilts, the cathedral treasury is a "house within a house." Via an asymmetrical staircase, visitors reach the upper floor, while small footbridges lead them to the "casket." The highlight of this tour is the elevated cathedral treasury that maintains a respectful distance to the venerable structure, allowing for an elegant, functional, and

moderne et attrayante. La façade, plus généreusement vitrée qu'auparavant, avec des fenêtres descendant jusqu'au sol, tout comme la nouvelle entrée, constituent désormais une vitrine appropriée, engageante, de l'église au cœur de la ville.

Après la transformation, le musée de la cathédrale se présente sous forme d'une succession de cabinets : neuf salles, dans l'aile sud du cloître, sont utilisées désormais pour l'exposition permanente, une salle supplémentaire ayant été aménagée pour les expositions temporaires. L'ancienne chapelle Sainte-Marguerite du cloître constitue la pièce centrale du musée. On y a supprimé la dalle intermédiaire installée après la seconde guerre mondiale, pour lui donner plus d'ampleur et produire plus d'effet. Reposant sur quatre poteaux, le Trésor est comme une « maison dans la maison », que les visiteurs atteignent par un escalier décalé par rapport à l'axe et un ensemble de passerelles. Point culminant du parcours, au sens propre et au figuré, à distance respectueuse des murs vénérables

Fenstern nun großzügiger als zuvor verglaste Fassade zeigt zusammen mit einem neuen Eingangsportal die Präsenz der kirchlichen Angebote im Stadtraum heute adäquater und einladender.

Die Situation des Dom-Museums nach dem Umbau gleicht einer Abfolge kabinettartiger, linearer Räume. Neun Räume am Südflügel des Kreuzgangs werden heute für die Dauerausstellung genutzt und zusätzlich wurde ein Raum für Sonderausstellungen geschaffen. Zentraler Ort des Museums ist die ehemalige Margarethenkapelle des Kreuzgangs, deren nach dem Zweiten Weltkrieg eingebaute Zwischendecke entfernt wurde, um dem Raum mehr Größe und damit Wirkung zu geben. Auf vier Stützen aufgeständert, steht die Domschatzkammer wie ein „Haus im Haus" im Raum. Über eine aus der Achse heraus geschobene Treppe gelangen die Besucher in das obere Stockwerk und über Stege zur „Schatulle": Höhepunkt des Rundgangs ist diese aufgeständerte Domschatzkammer, die respektvollen Abstand zu den altehrwürdigen Gemäuern hält

modern exhibition design. The carefully chosen objects are seen to great effect in front of a black backdrop.

In the courtyard, a new building was designed with an ellipsoidal ground plan which is used as rehearsal space for choirs. It is separated from the existing building but is easily accessible by a glazed corridor. In geometric terms, the structure resembles a diagonally cut transverse-oval truncated cone. It has been carefully integrated into the church garden that lies behind the cathedral.

qui l'abritent, il atteste d'une mise en scène moderne, élégante et efficace. La présentation sur un fond noir met les objets précieux particulièrement bien en valeur.

Dans la cour, sur un plan elliptique, on a construit un nouveau bâtiment pour les répétitions des chorales. Il est détaché des bâtiments existants, mais est accessible à l'abri des intempéries par une galerie vitrée. La construction est un tronc de cône, coupé selon un plan incliné dessinant une ellipse, soigneusement intégré dans le jardin à l'arrière de la cathédrale.

und eine elegante, wirkungsvolle und moderne Ausstellungsinszenierung erlaubt. Vor einem schwarzen Hintergrund kommen die erlesenen Objekte gut zur Geltung.

Auf einem ellipsenförmigen Grundriss entstand im Hof ein Neubau, der als Probenraum für Chöre genutzt wird. Er steht vom Gebäudebestand abgelöst, ist aber über einen gläsernen Gang trockenen Fußes zu erreichen. Geometrisch gleicht der Bau einem schräg abgeschnittenen, querovalen Kegelstumpf. Er ist sorgfältig in den hinter dem Dom liegenden Kirchgarten integriert.

OFFICE OF THE ARCHITECTURE FIRM BAUER, LUXEMBOURG (L)

CABINET D'ARCHITECTURE BAUER, LUXEMBOURG (L)
ARCHITEKTURBÜRO BAUER, LUXEMBURG (L)

An architect's office is expected to be the spatial visiting card for the firm. Like a microcosm it represents the office's outlook and taste, taking clients, co-workers, and guests on an aesthetic tour of the design concept of the office's founders and directors. Christian Bauer's office is set back from the street and lies in a formerly rather featureless district of Luxembourg, which has since become trendy. The fact that the building is a converted old warehouse is not immediately recognizable.

The design's objective was to turn the existing building into a meaningful urban anchor located in an otherwise fragmented environment by using simple tools and techniques. The original building was stripped of its later additions and all its non-structural walls inside and brought back to its original oblong shape, which included a saddle roof.

The load-bearing structure was only altered where there was a need to create new visual relationships. The second and third floors, for example, are connected by an air space. Daylight enters the space through a centrally placed incision in the ceiling, which also houses an elegant staircase.

The façades were hardly changed. Only the window parapets were removed to allow for larger openings. A large new window that forms the rear "garden façade" provides views into the interiors and from the foyer into the garden.

Le bâtiment qui abrite le cabinet est la carte de visite de tout architecte. Tel un microcosme, il reflète sa posture et ses goûts et il fait pénétrer de la même manière clients, collaborateurs et visiteurs dans le monde esthétique du « patron ». Le cabinet de Christian Bauer se trouve en retrait de la rue, dans un quartier de Luxembourg autrefois sans prétention, aujourd'hui en vogue. Ce n'est qu'à la deuxième lecture qu'on s'aperçoit qu'il s'agit en fait d'un ancien entrepôt transformé en bureaux.

L'objectif du projet était, avec des moyens simples, d'amarrer le bâtiment existant dans son environnement urbain fragmenté. Le bâtiment original, débarrassé des ajouts plus tardifs et de toutes les cloisons intérieures, en quelque sorte nettoyé, a retrouvé sa forme parallélépipédique originale, avec une toiture à deux pans. Les interventions au niveau de la structure portante ont été limitées au strict nécessaire, afin de créer de nouvelles liaisons visuelles. Le premier et le deuxième étage sont reliés par exemple par des « incisions » pratiquées dans la trame centrale du plancher intermédiaire. Elles ouvrent le passage à la lumière naturelle et l'une d'elles accueille un élégant escalier.

Les façades ont été à peine modifiées. Seules les allèges ont été éliminées, pour agrandir les ouvertures. Une nouvelle fenêtre, de dimensions généreuses, a été percée dans la façade sur jardin, à l'arrière, et

Das eigene Büro ist die Visitenkarte eines jeden Architekten. Wie ein Mikrokosmos steht es für seine Haltung und seinen Geschmack und entführt Kunden, Mitarbeiter und Gäste gleichermaßen in die gestalterische Welt des Namensgebers. Das Büro von Christian Bauer liegt von der Straße zurückgesetzt in einem ehemals einfachen, heute angesagten Stadtteil von Luxemburg. Dass es sich bei dem Gebäude um ein umgebautes altes Lagerhaus handelt, erkennt man erst auf den zweiten Blick.

Ziel des Entwurfs war es, mit einfachen Mitteln ein Bestandsgebäude zum Anker in seinem städtebaulich fragmentierten Umfeld zu machen. Das Originalgebäude wurde von seinen späteren Anbauten und allen nichttragenden Trennwänden im Inneren befreit und so gewissermaßen „gereinigt" und auf seine ursprüngliche längsrechteckige Form mit Satteldach zurückgeführt. In das Tragwerk wurde nur eingegriffen, wo das nötig war, um neue Sichtbeziehungen zu schaffen. Das erste und zweite Obergeschoss beispielsweise wurden durch einen Luftraum miteinander verbunden. Durch den mittigen Schnitt in die Geschossdecke dringt heute natürliches Tageslicht in den Raum. In diesem Ausschnitt liegt auch eine elegante Treppe.

Die Fassaden wurden kaum verändert, allein die Fensterbrüstungen wurden entfernt, um größere Öffnungen zu ermöglichen. Ein

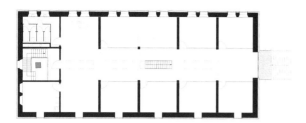 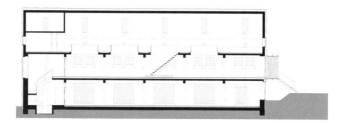

An exclusive range of carefully chosen materials is used in the interiors, as can be seen in the wooden floors, the glass partition walls and glass parapets. The built-in furniture, such as the wall-high book shelves, was specially manufactured from colored medium-density fiberboards, which simultaneously serve as spatial dividers. The old wooden roof was replaced by a solid roof with long vertical window openings. All façades as well as the roof, acting as "fifth façade," were additionally insulated. The new façade skin is black and was clad with a delicate horizontal frame made of untreated larch wood. This wooden cocoon underlines and unifies the geometry of the building. The façade recalls images of the wooden garden houses in the neighborhood.

A small room is located in front of the building, shaped by the fire wall of the neighboring building. It is today being used as advertising space by the company that has rented the first floor. A bamboo frame carries a green wall of creepers that separates the public from the more private spaces. The car park has a surface covering of gray chippings that creates a contrast to the wooden façade and the plants.

permet des vues sur celui-ci depuis les espaces intérieurs, et notamment le hall.

Les locaux intérieurs font intervenir un petit nombre de matériaux de choix : bois pour les sols, verre pour les cloisons et les allèges. Tout le mobilier intégré, telles les étagères qui font toute la hauteur du mur et servent en même temps de cloisons séparatives, a été fabriqué sur mesure en panneaux MDF teints dans la masse. L'ancienne charpente en bois a été remplacée par une charpente en béton fendue de longues baies dans le sens de la pente. Les façades et la toiture – « cinquième façade » – ont reçu une isolation extérieure supplémentaire et la nouvelle peau du bâtiment, noire, a été revêtue par un fin lattis horizontal en mélèze non traité. Ce cocon en bois souligne la géométrie du bâtiment et l'unifie. Il rappelle également les abris de jardin, en bois, du voisinage.

Devant le bâtiment, un petit espace, délimité par les contreforts de la maison voisine, sert d'espace publicitaire à l'entreprise qui loue le rez-de-chaussée. Un treillage en tiges de bambou supporte un « mur vert » de plantes grimpantes et sépare la partie publique de la partie privée. Le parking est traité en gravillons gris qui contrastent avec la façade en bois et la végétation.

neues, großzügiges Fenster als rückwärtige Gartenfassade erlaubt Blicke von den Interieurs und selbst vom Foyer aus in den Garten.

Die Innenräume sind mit wenigen ausgewählten Materialien gestaltet: Holzfußböden und gläserne Trennwände sowie -brüstungen. Alle Einbaumöbel wie zum Beispiel die wandgroßen Bücherregale wurden aus eingefärbten MDF-Platten maßgefertigt. Sie dienen zugleich als Raumteiler. Das ehemalige Holzdach wurde durch ein Massivdach mit langen vertikalen Fensteröffnungen ersetzt. Alle Fassaden und ebenso das Dach als „fünfte Fassade" wurden außen zusätzlich isoliert. Die neue Fassadenhaut ist schwarz und wurde mit einem feinen, horizontalen Stabwerk aus unbehandelter Lärche verkleidet. Dieser hölzerne Kokon betont und vereinheitlicht die Geometrie des Hauses. Die Holzfassade ist eine Anspielung auf die ebenfalls hölzernen Gartenhäuser der Umgebung.

Vor dem Gebäude liegt ein kleiner Raum, der von der Brandwand des Nachbarhauses geprägt wird. Sie wird heute als Reklamefläche von der Firma genutzt, die das Erdgeschoss gemietet hat. Ein Gerüst aus Bambusstäben trägt eine grüne Wand aus Kletterpflanzen, die den öffentlichen von dem privateren Bereich trennt. Die Autoabstellflächen haben einen Belag aus grauem Splitt, der als Kontrast zu der Holzfassade

OFFICE BUILDING JEAN SCHMIT ENGINEERING, LUXEMBURG (L)

BUREAU D'ÉTUDES JEAN SCHMIT ENGINEERING, LUXEMBOURG (L)
INGENIEURBÜRO JEAN SCHMIT ENGINEERING, LUXEMBURG (L)

For any architect, the chance to design a building for a client with a pronounced understanding of architecture is a particular joy and a welcome challenge. The engineering consultancy Jean Schmit Engineering is, indeed, such an ideal client: christian bauer & associés architectes have converted an existing building for the headquarters of this environmental engineering company, giving it a new architectural identity.

The rust-colored CorTen© steel façade changes to a matt brown hue and sometimes even glows in a warm orange color, depending on the incidence of sunlight. The colors and materials used are unique for the upper middle-class district of Belair where the office is located.

The building is divided into four sections: the first floor, adjacent to the street, houses the assembly rooms. Alongside, a long passage leads to the office spaces located at the rear. The main building is set back and consists of an historical building and of a new wing located in the front. A courtyard connects the two parts. The new wing is also accessible through the front building, amalgamating the four parts into one whole.

The architecture is inspired by and retains the particularities of the existing building. It

Construire pour des clients qui connaissent particulièrement bien l'architecture, c'est pour tout architecte à la fois une joie et un défi. Le bureau d'études Jean Schmit Engineering était donc un client rêvé : pour le siège social de ce bureau d'études en génie technique, cba a ainsi transformé un bâtiment existant pour lui donner une nouvelle identité architecturale.

La façade en acier CorTen© couleur rouille paraît, au gré de l'éclairement du soleil, brune et éteinte ou orange et vive. Tant la couleur que le matériau sont inhabituels dans ce quartier bourgeois de Belair où se trouve le bureau.

Celui-ci est organisé aujourd'hui en quatre ensembles. Au rez-de-chaussée, le long de la rue, se trouvent les salles de réunion, séparées des bureaux à l'arrière par un long passage. Le bâtiment principal, en retrait, se compose d'une construction ancienne et d'un nouvel ensemble à l'avant, tous deux étant reliés par une cour intérieure couverte. Le nouveau bâtiment est à son tour raccordé à l'avant-corps, de sorte que les quatre ensembles forment un tout.

L'architecture a entièrement misé sur les qualités de l'existant. Celui-ci a été vidé et sa structure dégagée, le projet se conten-

Für Kunden mit ausgeprägtem Architekturverständnis zu bauen, ist für jeden Architekten eine Freude und Herausforderung. Das Ingenieurbüro Jean Schmit Engineering ist so ein Traumkunde: Für den Hauptsitz der Haustechnikingenieure haben christian bauer & associés architectes ein Bestandsgebäude umgebaut und ihm eine neue architektonische Identität gegeben:

Die rostrote CorTen©-Stahlfassade des Büros wirkt je nach Sonneneinfall stumpf-braun oder leuchtend warm-orange. Farbton und Material sind untypisch für das gutbürgerliche Wohnviertel Belair, in dem das Büro liegt.

Das Haus ist in vier Teile gegliedert: Im Erdgeschoss an der Straße befinden sich die Versammlungsräume. Eine lang gestreckte Passage führt daran vorbei zu den rückwärtigen Büros. Das zurückgesetzte Hauptgebäude besteht aus einem Altbau sowie aus einem vorgelagerten neuen Block und einem Innenhof, der beide miteinander verbindet. Der neue Block ist auch an das Vorderhaus angeschlossen, sodass die vier Elemente ein Ganzes bilden.

Die Architektur setzt ganz auf die Qualitäten des Bestands. Die überformte Originalsubstanz wurde ausgeräumt und ihre Struktur

was stripped of its later additions and hollowed out, laying bare its inner structure. The new design serves to amplify the qualities of the original building. The load-bearing beams, for example, were merely extended and new floors added in the same spirit as the old ones. A series of coal-dust bricks were used to recreate the original rhythm of the windows. The use of steel restores the balanced relationship between inside and outside: inside, steel beams are used, on the outside a steel façade.

The building was converted using recycled materials only. The entire building was thermally insulated, the windows double-glazed. Together with the green roof, this exemplifies the company headquarters' ecological outlook.

tant d'en souligner le caractère. Les poutres ont simplement été prolongées et les étages complétés. Pour rétablir le rythme des fenêtres, un rang de briques a été ajouté. L'utilisation de l'acier établit un lien entre l'intérieur et l'extérieur : à l'intérieur, il est présent sous forme de poutrelles métalliques, à l'extérieur, il habille la façade.

On n'a pas utilisé d'autres matériaux que ceux qui avaient déjà été utilisés auparavant. L'ensemble du bâtiment a été isolé, des fenêtres à double vitrage ont été installées et les toitures végétalisées. De la sorte, le siège de ce bureau d'études en génie climatique devenait en même temps l'emblème de son approche écologique.

freigelegt. Der Entwurf verstärkt das Bestehende nur. Die Träger beispielsweise wurden lediglich verlängert und die Geschosse weitergedacht. Eine Reihe Brennziegel wurde hinzugefügt, um den Rhythmus der Fenster wieder herzustellen. Die Verwendung von Stahl stellt den Zusammenhang zwischen innen und außen her: innen in Form von Stahlträgern und außen als Fassade.

Es kam nur Material zur Anwendung, das bereits früher benutzt worden war. Das gesamte Gebäude wurde thermisch isoliert, die Fenster doppelt verglast und die Dächer begrünt, damit der Sitz des Klimaingenieurs zugleich Ausweis seines ökologischen Denkens wird.

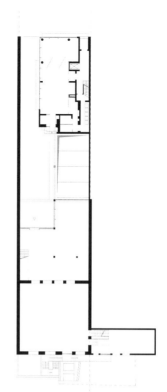

FACTORY SHED FOR ROTAREX, ECHTERNACH (L)

ATELIER DE FABRICATION ROTAREX, ECHTERNACH (L)
FABRIKATIONSHALLE ROTAREX, ECHTERNACH (L)

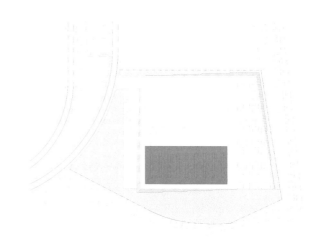

At the city limits of Echternach, in the middle of a green field, there stands a factory shed which was originally built for the Rotarex company, looking like a minimalist cube set in a hilly landscape. The large hall rests on a podium made of coarse cobblestones packed into gabions. This podium forms an archaic-looking contrast to the high-tech appearance of the hall and recalls images of the vineyards in the vicinity. Shimmering metal façade panels clad the walls of the cube, appearing to be seamless. The plain-looking façades have a limited number of slits incised into them. Even the edges of the large gates seem as if they have been cut into the façade with a knife.

A hot-dip galvanized steel table forms the entrance to the office wing. The northeastern façade is entirely glass-clad and looks

L'atelier de fabrication, construit à l'origine pour l'entreprise Rotarex, est situé en pleine nature, en bordure de la ville d'Echternach, cube minimaliste dans un paysage vallonné. Il repose sur une plate-forme en gabions remplis de grosses pierres ramassées dans les champs. Cette monumentale estrade constitue un contre-point primitif à l'expression moderne et high-tech de l'atelier, clin d'œil aux vignobles proches. Des panneaux de façade métalliques, chatoyants, habillent les murs d'une peau semble-t-il sans coutures. Les façades, planes, sont percées d'ouvertures minimales, réduites à leur plus stricte nécessité. Les arêtes des grandes portes paraissent elles aussi taillées au couteau dans la façade.

Corps métallique poli, l'atelier semble s'inscrire en contrepoint dans le paysage. Un

Am Stadtrand von Echternach, „auf der grünen Wiese", steht die ursprünglich für die Firma Rotarex gebaute Fabrikationshalle wie ein minimalistischer Kubus in der hügeligen Landschaft. Die große Halle ruht auf einem Podium aus groben Feldsteinen in Gabionen. Dieses Podest setzt gegen den modernen Hightech-Ausdruck der Halle einen archaischen Kontrapunkt, der auf die nahen Weinberge anspielt. Metallisch schimmernde Fassadenpaneele bekleiden die fugenlos wirkenden Wände des geschliffenen Kubus. Die flächigen Fassaden haben lediglich notwendige Schlitze. Selbst die Kanten der großen Tore scheinen wie mit dem Messer in die Fassade geschnitten.

Ein feuerverzinkter Stahltisch bildet den Eingang zum Bürotrakt. Die Nord-Ost-Fassade ist völlig verglast und wirkt wie ein riesiger

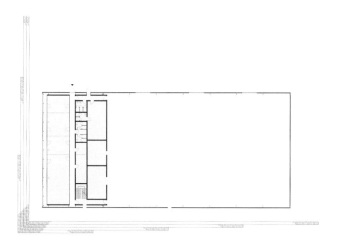

like a giant wide-angle screen. The office wing is placed behind it. The lettering and logo of Rotarex can be seen on the upper left corner of the façade, much like on a television screen.

The thoughtful and convincing arrangement of all the individual parts creates an austere, geometrical building that produces strong contrasts between an archaic appearance and high technology, as well as between architecture and nature.

auvent, table monumentale en acier galvanisé, marque l'entrée de la partie bureau. La face nord-est, entièrement vitrée, se présente comme un immense écran derrière lequel s'abritent les bureaux. Et comme sur un écran, le nom et le logo de l'entreprise Rotarex s'y inscrivent en haut à gauche. Convaincante, la disposition intelligente des différentes composantes de cet ensemble se traduit par un bâtiment à la géométrie stricte, avec un contraste fort entre rusticité et technicité, entre architecture et nature.

Breitwandbildschirm. Dahinter befindet sich der Bürotrakt. Wie auf einem Fernsehbild sind Schriftzug und Logo der Firma Rotarex oben links auf der Fassade zu sehen.

Die intelligente und überzeugende Anordnung der Einzelteile ergibt einen strengen, geometrischen Baukörper und schafft einen starken Kontrast zwischen Archaik und Hochtechnologie, Baukunst und Natur.

EUROPEAN SCHOOL, LUXEMBOURG (L)

ÉCOLE EUROPÉENNE, LUXEMBOURG (L)
EUROPASCHULE, LUXEMBURG (L)

The European School in Luxembourg is a true, albeit unintentional, image of the European Union. Here, children from almost every European country play and learn together, exemplifying pan-European life to the adults. The school, located on the Kirchberg plateau on which most EU institutions in Luxembourg have their headquarters, is itself a child of the EU: it was founded to teach the children of the EU's public servants in their respective country's language. With every extension of the EU, the school became more international and finally, too small to provide adequate facilities. With its 4,200 students who are taught in eleven languages, the school is today the largest of all European schools. Twenty-four European languages are part of the teaching schedule that promotes multilingual, multicultural, and multiconfessional lessons from kindergarten to the school-leaving examinations.

The original buildings were constructed in the spirit of the nineteen-seventies: the free-standing buildings are set back from the boulevard Konrad Adenauer and stand like a barricade of wagons that unfortunately fail to constructively shape the street spaces on the Kirchberg plateau or to urbanize this "elephant graveyard of modern architecture."

When Christian Bauer was asked to build an extension for the school, he took the opportunity to invert the urban paradigm the origi-

L'École européenne de Luxembourg est à l'image de l'Union européenne. Comment pourrait-il en être autrement ? Les enfants de presque tous les pays européens y jouent et y apprennent ensemble, montrant aux adultes l'exemple de ce qu'est la vie « paneuropéenne » au quotidien. L'école, située sur le plateau de Kirchberg, où la plupart des institutions de l'Union Européenne installées au Luxembourg ont leur siège, est elle-même fille de l'Union : elle fut créée pour que les enfants des fonctionnaires européens puissent poursuivre leur scolarité dans leur langue nationale respective. À chaque nouvel élargissement de l'Union, elle devenait toujours plus internationale, mais aussi toujours plus à l'étroit dans ses murs. Avec ses 4200 élèves, répartis en onze sections linguistiques, elle est aujourd'hui la plus importante de toutes les écoles européennes. Le programme pédagogique, qui affiche 24 langues européennes, prévoit un enseignement plurilingue, pluriculturel et pluriconfessionnel, de la maternelle jusqu'au baccalauréat.

Les bâtiments initiaux étaient dans l'esprit des années 1970 : en retrait par rapport au boulevard Konrad Adenauer, dispersés, ils ne parvenaient pas à donner forme au boulevard ni à urbaniser ce « cimetière d'éléphants » de l'architecture moderne.

Sollicité pour réaliser l'extension de l'école, Christian Bauer a saisi cette opportunité

Die Europaschule in Luxemburg ist ein – unbeabsichtigtes – Abbild der Europäischen Union: Hier spielen und lernen die Kinder aus fast allen europäischen Ländern miteinander und machen den Erwachsenen das paneuropäische Leben im Alltag vor. Die Schule auf dem Kirchberg-Plateau, auf dem die meisten EU-Institutionen in Luxemburg ihren Sitz haben, ist selbst ein Kind der EU: Gegründet, um die Kinder der EU-Beamten in ihrer jeweiligen Landessprache zu unterrichten, wurde sie mit jeder Erweiterung der EU internationaler – und letztlich zu klein. Mit ihren 4200 Schülern, die in elf Sprachsektionen unterrichtet werden, ist die Schule heute die größte aller Europaschulen. 24 europäische Sprachen stehen auf dem Unterrichtsplan, der mehrsprachigen, multikulturellen und -konfessionellen Unterricht vom Kindergarten bis zum Abitur vorsieht.

Die ursprünglichen Bauten folgten dem Geist der siebziger Jahre: Zurückgesetzt vom Boulevard Konrad Adenauer stehen sie wie eine Wagenburg aus Solitären und helfen nicht dabei, die Straßenräume auf dem Kirchberg-Plateau zu formen oder diesen „Elefantenfriedhof der modernen Architektur" zu urbanisieren.

Als Christian Bauer gebeten wurde, die Schule zu erweitern, nutzte er die Chance, die städtebauliche Haltung der Ursprungsbauten in ihr Gegenteil zu verkehren: Er

nal buildings had been constructed in: he placed the two most important wings of the school, the primary and secondary schools, in long three-story strips housing the classrooms along the road. This simple arrangement had a double advantage: it creates a protected school yard on the one hand and a clearly legible street space on the other. The administrative section and the prominently placed oval community hall lie between both wings, symbolically linking both schools. Towards the courtyard, the façades of the foyer are dissolved into a grid of small squares. The triple flight stairs offer ample opportunities to see and be seen.

Out of the seven buildings that were once built for the European School, three have been demolished to make way for more urban successors. Two new buildings directly connect to the existing ones: there is the long bar-shaped building that houses the secondary school and the cafeteria that nestles to an existing flat building in the shape

pour renverser le parti urbanistique initial et caler les deux principaux corps de bâtiment, qui abritent les classes du primaire et du secondaire, le long de la voie, en longues bandes de type R+2. Cette disposition astucieuse, toute simple, présente un double intérêt : elle permet à la fois de créer une cour de récréation à l'abri des bâtiments et de donner de la lisibilité côté boulevard. Entre les deux corps se logent le bâtiment administratif et la salle polyvalente de forme elliptique, qui occupe ainsi une place de choix, reliant symboliquement les deux cycles de scolarité. Côté cour, les façades des halls d'accueil sont percées en petites trames carrées. Quant aux escaliers à trois volées, ils offrent des espaces pour voir et être vu.

Des sept bâtiments construits initialement, trois ont été démolis pour laisser place aux nouvelles constructions, plus urbaines. Deux de ces nouvelles constructions se greffent directement sur des bâtiments existants : la

platzierte die beiden wichtigsten Flügel der Schule, die Grund- und die Oberschule, in langen dreistöckigen Bändern für die Klassentrakte entlang der Straße. Dieser einfache Kunstgriff hat doppelten Nutzen: Er schafft einen geschützten Schulhof auf der einen und einen lesbaren Straßenraum auf der anderen Seite. Zwischen beiden Flügeln liegen der Verwaltungstrakt und der prominent platzierte, ovale Gemeinschaftssaal, der symbolisch beide Schulen miteinander verbindet. Zum Hof hin sind die Fassaden der Foyers in kleine Quadratraster aufgelöst. Die dreiläufigen Treppen bieten Raum zum Sehen und Gesehenwerden.

Von den sieben Gebäuden, die einst für die Europaschule gebaut wurden, wurden drei abgerissen, um Platz zu machen für die urbaneren Nachfolgerbauten. Zwei Neubauten schließen direkt an Bestandsgebäude an: der lange Riegel des Gymnasiums und die Cafeteria, die sich in Form eines Viertelovals an einen bestehenden Flachbau anschmiegt.

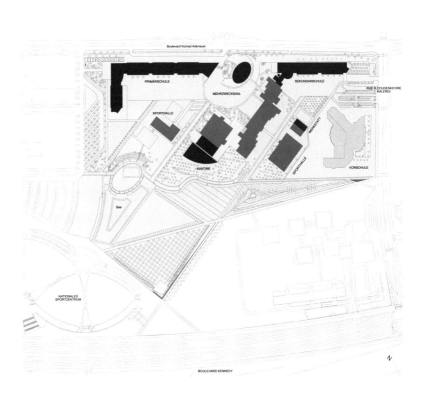

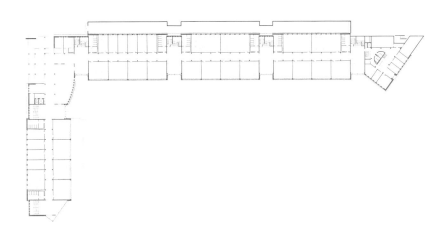

of a quarter oval. The three most important buildings are directly accessible from the street. The wing housing the classrooms is an oblong block-like building, while the special spaces such as the auditorium and the cafeteria have softer shapes. Like the architecture, the color concept is also rather expressive: while the classroom wing is marked by exposed concrete, the windows and doors of the classrooms have signal colors that facilitate easy orientation and recognition. The higher-placed auditorium has a reddish façade and a central oculus that admits zenithal light into the auditorium, reminiscent of the pantheon in Rome.

grande barre du lycée et la cantine, un quart d'ellipse qui se presse contre un bâtiment bas existant. Les trois bâtiments principaux sont tous trois accessibles directement depuis la rue. Les bâtiments abritant les salles de classe sont des parallélépipèdes aux formes strictes tandis que les locaux tels la salle polyvalente ou la cantine ont des formes arrondies. Les couleurs sont appliquées par touches : les bâtiments de cours sont en béton apparent, avec des accents colorés pour les fenêtres et les portes des salles de classe, ce qui facilite l'identification et l'orientation. La salle polyvalente, plus haute que les autres bâtiments, a une façade dans des tons rouges et un oculus central qui, presque comme au Panthéon à Rome, laisse pénétrer la lumière zénithale.

Die drei wichtigsten Gebäude sind direkt von der Straße aus zugänglich. Die Klassentrakte sind als Riegel ausgebildet, die Sonderräume wie Aula und Cafeteria haben weichere Formen. Auch das Farbkonzept setzt Akzente: Während die Klassentrakte von Sichtbeton geprägt sind, haben die Fenster und Türen der Klassenzimmer Signalfarben, die die Orientierung und damit auch die Identifikation erleichtern. Die höhere Aula hat eine rötliche Fassade und ein zentrales Okulus, das fast wie im Pantheon in Rom zenitales Licht in die Aula fallen lässt.

SES HEADQUARTERS, BETZDORF (L)

SIÈGE SOCIAL SES, BETZDORF (L)

HAUPTSITZ DER FIRMA SES, BETZDORF (L)

As owner of the Astra satellite system, SES (Société Européenne des Satellites) and its fourty-one satellites reach around 95 percent of the world's population. The company also has stakes in satellite-operating companies in Asia, Latin America, and Scandinavia and in satellite technology firms. Commercially successful, SES goes back to a pan-European initiative. This not only makes it one of the most well-known employers in Luxembourg but also a symbol for successful pan-European cooperation.

The design for SES's headquarters was the result of a design competition that was held in 1997, with the architects being faced with the challenge of finding a suitable built-form. Taking inspiration from ring-shaped satellite orbits, the architects decided to use a two-story ring shape for the building.

The SES headquarters have been harmoniously integrated into the sensitive natural environment: a small castle, the Château de Betzdorf and a large company-owned satellite complex are located on a large forested site set in a hilly landscape. The château, formerly belonging to the grand duke of Luxembourg, is used for conferences and company events. The ring-shaped new building, near the castle, is built almost entirely on stilts to leave the largest possible area free of construction. The building houses all

La société SES (Société Européenne des Satellites), propriétaire du système de satellites Astra, touche environ 95 pourcent de la population mondiale grâce à ses 41 satellites. SES détient également des participations dans d'autres opérateurs de satellites en Asie, en Amérique latine et en Scandinavie ainsi que dans des sociétés de technologie satellitaire. Fruit d'une initiative européenne, la société n'a cessé de remporter des succès commerciaux, ce qui fait d'elle non seulement un des employeurs les plus connus du Luxembourg, mais aussi le symbole d'une coopération paneuropéenne réussie.

Le projet pour le siège social de SES est le résultat d'un concours qui s'est déroulé en 1997 et pour lequel les architectes ambitionnaient de trouver une image adaptée. Les satellites décrivant des orbites autour de la terre, c'est l'anneau, sur deux niveaux, qui s'est tout naturellement imposé pour le bâtiment.

Le siège de SES s'intègre harmonieusement dans un environnement naturel sensible. Un petit château, le Château de Betzdorf, et un grand parc d'antennes de la société sont implantés sur le vaste terrain couvert de forêt, dans un paysage vallonné. Le château, autrefois possession du Grand-Duc du Luxembourg, est utilisé pour

Die Firma SES (Société Européenne des Satellites) erreicht als Eigner des Astra-Satellitensystems mit ihren 41 Satelliten etwa 95 Prozent der Weltbevölkerung. Das Unternehmen hält zusätzlich Beteiligungen an Satellitenbetreibern in Asien, Lateinamerika und Skandinavien und ist an Unternehmen der Satellitentechnologie beteiligt. SES gründet auf einer europäischen Initiative und ist kommerziell sehr erfolgreich. Das macht sie nicht nur zu einem der bekanntesten Arbeitgeber in Luxemburg, sondern auch zu einem Symbol für erfolgreiche paneuropäische Zusammenarbeit.

Der Entwurf für den Hauptsitz der SES ging 1997 aus einem Wettbewerb hervor. Ehrgeiz der Architekten war es, ein geeignetes bauliches Bild zu finden. Da die Satelliten die Erde in einer Ringform umkreisen, lag es nahe, auch für das Gebäude eine zweigeschossige Ringform zu verwenden.

Der SES-Hauptsitz wurde harmonisch in die sensible natürliche Umgebung integriert: Auf dem weitläufigen Waldgrundstück befinden sich in einer hügeligen Landschaft ein kleines Schloss, das Château de Betzdorf, und eine große, firmeneigene Satellitenanlage. Das Château, ehemals ein Gut des Großherzogs von Luxemburg, wird für Konferenzen und Veranstaltungen der SES genutzt. Der Ring des Neubaus nahe dem Schloss ist fast

departments on two levels. Its shape makes a flexible spatial organization possible. The aluminium façades have vertical ventilation lobes with protective louvers. Balconies that serve as escape routes double as sun-shading elements.

A multipurpose center, called MPC for short, can be used for company-facilitated sports activities and large gatherings such as company parties or meetings of shareholders. To more smoothly integrate the MPC into the complex, it has been embedded into the site to a large extent and is naturally lit by skylights.

An elevated platform serves as connector between the castle and the new building. Half-sunk into the ground, it opens up towards the valley and houses the technical and multipurpose spaces, as well as the kitchen and the restaurant. A garden, acting as buffer between the forest and the lawn, conveniently hides the parking lot where there is space for future extensions of the building.

des conférences et des manifestations de SES. L'anneau du nouveau bâtiment, près du château, est juché sur de légers pilotis sur presque tout son tracé, pour dégager au maximum le terrain. Il héberge l'ensemble des départements de la société sur deux niveaux. Sa forme permet une organisation spatiale flexible. Les façades à ossature aluminium comportent des volets d'aération verticaux, avec ventelles pare-pluie. Des plates-formes de secours servent en même temps de brise-soleil.

Une « galette » aux murs légèrement incurvés fait le lien entre le château et l'anneau du nouveau bâtiment. Semi-enterrée, elle s'ouvre sur la vallée et abrite les locaux techniques et de service, tels la cuisine et le restaurant. On y jouit d'une vue sur les prairies de la vallée proche. Un jardin – espace tampon entre la forêt et la prairie – dissimule le parking réservé pour une extension ultérieure.

Une salle polyvalente (*Multipurpose Center*) peut être utilisée pour des activités sportives internes ou servir pour des grands rassemblements, fêtes de l'entreprise ou réunions des actionnaires, par exemple. Pour éviter que le volume de cette salle ne s'impose exagérément, elle se fond dans le terrain, bénéficiant d'un éclairage naturel par d'importants bandeaux vitrés au sommet des murs.

vollständig auf leichten Pilotis aufgeständert, um das Grundstück so weit wie möglich unverbaut zu belassen. Der Baukörper umfasst alle Abteilungen auf zwei Ebenen. Seine Form ermöglicht eine flexible räumliche Organisation. Die Fassaden aus Aluminium haben vertikale Lüftungsflügel mit Lamellen als Wetterschutz. Fluchtbalkone dienen zugleich als Sonnenschutzelemente.

Eine MPC (*Multipurpose Center*) genannte Halle kann für Betriebssport und große Zusammenkünfte wie Betriebsfeiern oder Aktionärsversammlungen verwendet werden. Um das Volumen des MPC nicht zu dominant wirken zu lassen, ist es größtenteils in das Gelände eingefügt und über Oberlicht-Laternen natürlich belichtet.

Ein Plateau mit leicht geschwungenen Wänden dient als Bindeglied zwischen dem Schloss und dem Neubau. Halb im Boden versenkt, öffnet es sich zum Tal und nimmt die Technik- und Mehrzweckräume, die Küche und das Restaurant auf. Ein Garten – als Puffer zwischen Wald und Wiese – versteckt den Parkplatz, wo zukünftig ein Erweiterungsbau errichtet werden könnte.

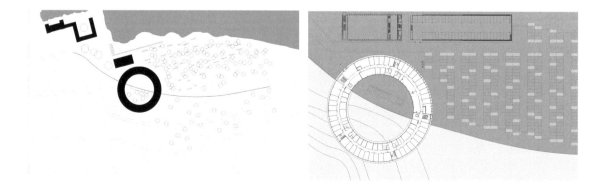

HOUSE IN BRIDEL-KAHLSCHEIER (L)

MAISON À BRIDEL-KAHLSCHEIER (L)
HAUS IN BRIDEL-KAHLSCHEIER (L)

This house was designed with a harmonious relationship between nature and architecture in mind. It skillfully makes use of the topography it finds itself in. The site, located on a slope, offers attractive views of the nearby valley. The architecture has been designed to make the most of the building's unique location, its views and the dense vegetation. Its geometrical outer appearance seems modest yet self-confident while its shape follows visual axes and the incidence of light, allowing for a loose arrangement of the spaces inside.

The change in the time of day and year can be suitably observed through panoramic windows that have been fitted in all the rooms. Horizontally placed wooden lagging, protected by a cantilevered roof, determines the look of the façade while the covered parking space has been built of exposed concrete. Its roof can be additionally used as a garden. Particularly elegant are the unclad building corners. The steel columns that carry the roof and the large band windows have not been disguised inside.

A dialog between materials and colors determines the design of the interiors. While ascending to the upper floor, residents and

Harmonie entre nature et architecture, tel était l'objectif fixé pour la maison de Bridel. Son volume use habilement de la topographie. Le terrain, en pente, offre des vues pittoresques sur la vallée proche et l'architecture tire le meilleur parti du site, des vues et de l'épaisse végétation. La géométrie extérieure de la maison s'affirme avec assurance, mais modestie. La forme est déterminée par les vues et la pénétration de la lumière et offre une succession informelle d'espaces intérieurs dont l'esthétique résulte d'un dialogue entre matériaux et couleurs.

Les fenêtres panoramiques permettent, depuis toutes les pièces, de suivre l'évolution du jour et la succession des saisons. Les façades sont habillées d'un bardage en bois horizontal protégé par le débord de la toiture, tandis que le garage ouvert est en béton apparent. La toiture-terrasse de celui-ci peut être utilisée en prolongement du jardin. Les angles du bâtiment sont vitrés, ce qui donne à la maison son élégance particulière. Les poteaux métalliques qui portent la toiture et permettent l'ouverture de bandeaux de fenêtres généreux, sont laissés visibles à l'intérieur.

Das Haus wurde im Hinblick auf die Harmonie zwischen Natur und Architektur hin entworfen. Sein Volumen nutzt geschickt die Topografie. Das Hanggrundstück bietet attraktive Ausblicke in das nahe Tal und die Architektur zieht den besten Nutzen aus der Lage, dem Ausblick und der dichten Vegetation. Bescheiden und doch selbstbewusst wirkt das geometrische Äußere; seine Form folgt Blickachsen und dem Lichteinfall und gibt eine lockere Anordnung der Innenräume vor.

Von allen Räumen aus lässt sich durch Panoramafenster der Wechsel der Tages- und Jahreszeiten verfolgen. Eine horizontale Holzverschalung, geschützt durch das auskragende Dach, prägt die Fassade, während der gedeckte Stellplatz in Sichtbeton gestaltet ist. Seine Überdachung kann als zusätzliche Gartenfläche genutzt werden. Besondere Eleganz gewinnt das Haus durch die unverkleideten Gebäudeecken. Die Stahlstützen, die das Dach tragen und die großzügigen Bandfenster erlauben, sind innen sichtbar belassen.

Ein Dialog der Materialien und Farben bestimmt die Gestaltung der Innenräume. Beim Aufstieg in das obere Geschoss haben

visitors look into a long corridor and at sliding walls that partition the spaces. A skylight admits daylight into the house. The window parapets have the same height as the tabletops of the built-in furniture. The floors are covered with parquet and crushed polygonal ceramic and natural stone tiles that give the interiors a sense of movement and dynamism.

Un long couloir lumineux s'ouvre à la vue des habitants et des visiteurs, ou au contraire s'escamote, au gré de l'ouverture et de la fermeture des cloisons coulissantes séparant une enfilade de pièces. Un étroit bandeau vitré au sommet des murs laisse pénétrer la lumière naturelle dans la pièce de vie. Les allèges de fenêtres ont la même hauteur que les plateaux du mobilier intégré. Parquet et dalles de pierre naturelle et de céramique, brisées en formes polygonales, animent les sols intérieurs.

Besucher und Bewohner einen Blick entlang eines weiten Flures und Schiebewänden, die die einzelnen Zimmer begrenzen. Durch eine Dachlaterne fällt natürliches Tageslicht in das Haus. Die Fensterbrüstungen haben dieselbe Höhe wie die Tischplatten der Einbaumöbel. Die Fußböden sind mit Parkett und polygonal gebrochenen Keramik- und Natursteinplatten belegt, die den Interieurs ein bewegtes Element verleihen.

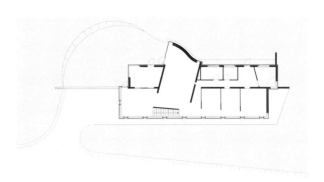

MOKO VILLA, SCHUTTRANGE (L)

MAISON MOKO, SCHUTTRANGE (L)
HAUS MOKO, SCHUTTRANGE (L)

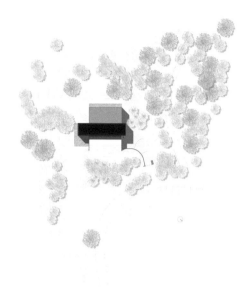

On a dreamy hill, on the outskirts of a forest, stands the "Moko" villa. Its exquisite wooden façades so perfectly blend with the landscape that one can be forgiven for thinking it has always been part of nature at this particular place. The design was guided by three premises: firstly, that the trees on the site would be protected as far as possible; secondly, that the building would be integrated seamlessly into the existing topography; and thirdly, that the wood which had been used in the construction of the small chalet on whose foundation the new building was erected, would be reused as building material. The overgrown, 6,000-square-meter-large site has been retained in its natural condition.

The sophistication with which the materials were chosen is evident everywhere,

Sur une colline idyllique au milieu de la forêt, à l'orée d'un bois touffu, la villa « Moko » se fond si parfaitement dans le paysage, avec ses précieux fronts en bois, qu'elle semble naturellement en faire partie. Trois idéesmaîtresses ont guidé le projet : les arbres présents sur le terrain devaient être conservés au maximum, le bâtiment devait s'insérer parfaitement dans la topographie du lieu et le bois du petit chalet existant, sur les fondations duquel la nouvelle maison devait être érigée, devait être réemployé pour la nouvelle construction. Le terrain de 6000 mètres carrés, à l'état sauvage, est resté intouché.

Dès le premier contact, le choix des graviers de la cour, dont la couleur s'harmonise avec le beige du calcaire bourguignon utilisé pour l'entrée, rend perceptible le sens aigu de la

Im Forst steht auf einem verträumten Hügel, am Rand eines dichten Waldsaums die Villa „Moko" – ein Gebäude, das sich mit seinen edlen Holzfronten so perfekt in die Landschaft schmiegt, dass man denkt, es gehöre von Natur aus hierher. Der Entwurf wurde von drei Maximen geleitet: Die Bäume auf dem Grundstück sollten weitestgehend erhalten, das Gebäude nahtlos in die gegebene Topografie eingefügt und das Holz jenes kleinen Chalets, das auf dem Areal stand und auf dessen Fundament das neue Haus errichtet werden sollte, als Baumaterial wiederverwendet werden. Das verwilderte, 6000 Quadratmeter große Grundstück wurde naturbelassen.

Der hoch entwickelte Sinn für Materialwirkungen zeigt sich bereits auf dem Boden – etwa bei der Wahl des Kiesbelags der Zufahrt,

starting from the gravel-covered driveway whose color resonates with the light yellow hue of the Burgundian stone used in the porch. Residents and visitors enter the villa through the large basement with its garage and from there ascend half a floor to the spacious residential pavilion that opens up to the natural surroundings on three sides with wall-high glazed façades. The kitchen is located directly next to the living and dining room, separated from it by built-in furniture. Apart from the all-glass parlor, the villa has a solid, down-to-earth foundation and a light wooden cube with French windows that looks like it has been superimposed on the structure below. The more private spaces, appearing like a wood-clad cocoon, are located here. Two half staircases lead residents from the living spaces into a corridor

matière et de ses effets que l'on retrouvera dans l'ensemble de la maison. On pénètre dans celle-ci par le grand sous-sol avec garage, d'où on monte d'un demi-niveau pour atteindre le vaste pavillon du séjour qui, vitré sur toute la hauteur, s'ouvre sur trois côtés sur la nature environnante. Masquée derrière le mobilier intégré, la cuisine s'accole à la salle de séjour et à la salle à manger.

Outre le salon vitré, la villa est constituée d'un soubassement solide, rustique, et d'un parallélépipède aérien en bois, avec des portes-fenêtres, qui semble simplement posé par-dessus. Il abrite, comme enveloppées d'un cocon de bois, les pièces les plus intimes de la maison. Deux demi-volées conduisent du séjour au couloir, qui dessert les chambres à coucher, les salles de bains

dessen Farbton mit dem hellgelben, burgundischen Stein im Windfang harmoniert.

Man betritt die Villa durch das große Souterrain mit Garage und steigt von dort ein halbes Stockwerk hinauf zum weitläufigen Wohnpavillon, der sich auf drei Seiten mit geschosshohen Glasfronten zur Natur öffnet. An den Wohn- und Speisesaal schließt sich, abgeschirmt durch Einbaumöbel, die Küche an.

Abgesehen von dem verglasten Salon besteht die Villa aus einer soliden, erdverbundenen Basis und einem leichten, wie darüber gestülpten Quader aus Holz mit französischen Fenstern. Hier liegen, wie in einen Kokon aus Holz gekleidet, die intimeren Räume. Zwei halbe Treppen führen vom Wohnbereich aus in den Gang von dem die Schlafzimmer, Bäder sowie

from which the bedrooms, bathrooms and the library can be reached. Maplewood parquet, ceiling claddings made of maple wood veneer, and light beige cotton curtains give the interiors a luster that is underlined by the interesting wooden patterns in the built structure. Ceilings, walls, built-in furniture, and floors harmonize with each other and have been planned down to the smallest detail. The wall facing the parlor is backlit, its frame-like structure filtering the light. Resonating with the color of the wood, warm white tones define the bathrooms and bedrooms.

ainsi que la bibliothèque. Le parquet en érable, le placage en érable des plafonds et les rideaux en coton écru confèrent aux intérieurs un certain éclat, encore renforcé par les nuances du bois. Les plafonds, murs, cloisons, mobilier intégré et sols s'harmonisent et ont été étudiés jusque dans le moindre détail. La claire-voie qui sépare le salon, éclairée par l'arrière, filtre la lumière. Dans les salles de bains et les chambres à coucher, des tonalités de blanc cassé contrastent avec le bois.

Le sol chauffant des salles de bains est revêtu de galets. Le bloc de cuisine est en Corian©.

die Bibliothek abzweigen. Ahornparkett, Deckenverkleidungen aus Ahornfurnier und Vorhänge aus hellbeiger Baumwolle verleihen den Interieurs einen Glanz, der durch die Variationen im Holzbau im Ausdruck noch gesteigert wird. Decken, Wände, Einbaumöbel und Böden harmonieren miteinander und sind bis ins kleinste Detail geplant. Die Wand zum Salon ist hinterleuchtet und filtert mit ihrem Stabwerk das Licht. Neben dem Holz setzen warme Weißtöne Akzente in den Bädern und Schlafzimmern.

In den Bädern bestehen die Böden aus Kieseln, die durch eine Fußbodenheizung er-

The floors in the bathrooms consist of pebbles that are heated by an under-floor heating system. The kitchen unit is made of Corian©. Exposed concrete, formed by rough sawn planks, defines the plinth walls. The external skin of the upper floor recalls the forest in the vicinity: an open-slat façade made of untreated larch wood wraps around the entire cube. Even the windows have been integrated into this structure. The glazed façade can turn into a maze of window shutters. It is only when nobody is at home and all shutters are closed that the cubical shape of the villa seems severe. During other times, the open shutters lend the building a playful dynamism. The semi-transparent skin provides views to the outside while simultaneously offering protection from curious glances. The external and internal façades seem like they are of one piece, seamlessly merging into each other.

Les soubassements de la maison, en béton apparent, ont été coffrés avec des planches brutes de sciage. L'enveloppe ajourée extérieure, à l'étage, constitue une référence à la forêt : en liteaux de mélèze laissés bruts, elle habille l'ensemble du parallélépipède, y compris les fenêtres, s'y transformant alors simplement en volets. Lorsque les habitants ont quitté la maison et que tous les volets sont fermés, alors seulement les volumes de la villa apparaissent dans toute leur rigueur. Le reste du temps, les volets ouverts lui confèrent une plasticité ludique. La semi-transparence de l'enveloppe préserve les vues sur l'extérieur tout en protégeant du regard des curieux. Claire-voie à l'extérieur, claire-voie à l'intérieur.

wärmt werden. Der Küchenblock ist aus Corian©. Sichtbeton, allerdings mit sägerauen Brettern geschalt, prägt die Sockelwände. Die Außenhülle des Obergeschosses stellt einen Bezug zum Wald her: Eine Lamellenfassade aus unbehandeltem Lärchenholz umfasst den ganzen Quader. Selbst die Fenster sind darin integriert: Vor den Glasflächen wird die Fassade einfach zum Fensterladen. Nur wenn niemand zu Hause ist und alle Läden geschlossen sind, wirken die kubischen Formen der Villa streng, andernfalls verleihen die aufgeklappten Läden dem Gebäude eine spielerische Plastizität. Die semi-transparente Hülle erlaubt Ausblicke und schützt dennoch vor neugierigen Einblicken. Außen- und Innenfassaden wirken wie aus einem Guss.

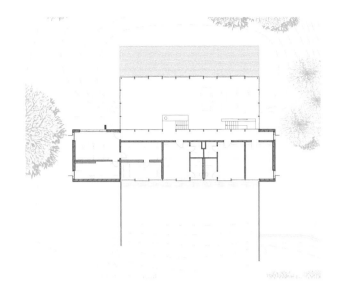

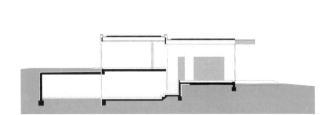

BAUER-RAFFAELLI HOUSE, LUXEMBOURG (L)

MAISON BAUER-RAFFAELLI, LUXEMBOURG (L)
HAUS BAUER-RAFFAELLI, LUXEMBURG (L)

The Bauer-Raffaelli villa has a simple oblong shape. Nevertheless, it has a refined spatial sophistication which, however, becomes apparent only after one has entered the building. It is located on the southern slope of the Kirchberg plateau, a location it uses to great effect by providing wide-angle views of the valley. Though facing the street and the neighboring building, the structure seems introverted only to open up towards the garden and the valley. The upper floor houses the private rooms, the basement the guest rooms. The first floor serves for living and dining purposes as well as for enjoying the displayed art.

The first and upper floor façades are clad with a glazed horizontal timber lathing of a black color reminiscent of traditional Japanese architecture. It rests on a base of exposed concrete on which rough sawn shuttering boards have left a horizontal pattern. As such, the villa looks like a dark wooden box placed on a plinth which has been embedded into the slope on the northern side. Large band windows on the upper floor and

Dans sa forme, la villa Bauer-Raffaelli a la simplicité du parallélépipède rectangle. Sa richesse, le raffinement de ses espaces intérieurs, ne se révèle qu'à celui qui pénètre dans la maison. Implantée sur le versant sud du plateau de Kirchberg, elle utilise habilement sa situation pour offrir des vues lointaines dans la vallée. Secrète côté rue ou vis-à-vis de ses voisines, elle n'en est que plus ouverte côté jardin et vallée. À l'étage, on trouve les pièces privées, au niveau inférieur les chambres d'amis et entre les deux, au rez-de-chaussée, le lieu où l'on vit et profite de la vie, où l'on nourrit corps et esprit. Les façades du rez-de-chaussée et de l'étage sont revêtues d'un lattis horizontal en bois lasuré noir, évocation de l'architecture japonaise traditionnelle. Elles reposent sur un soubassement en béton apparent où les planches brutes du coffrage ont également dessiné un motif horizontal. La villa semble ainsi être un coffre en bois sombre sur son socle, à moitié inscrit dans la pente au nord. Elle est percée de grandes fenêtres en bandeaux à l'étage, de portes-fenêtres au sous-

Die Villa Bauer-Raffaelli ist in ihrer Kubatur eine einfache längsrechteckige Box. Sie ist dennoch reich in ihrem räumlichen Raffinement, das sich nur dem erschließt, der das Haus betritt. Das Haus am Südhang des Kirchberg-Plateaus nutzt seine Lage am Hang geschickt für weite Blicke ins Tal. Zur Straße und zur Nachbarbebauung zeigt sich das Haus introvertiert, nur um sich zum Garten und zum Tal hin umso mehr zu öffnen. Im Obergeschoss befinden sich die Privaträume und im Untergeschoss die Gästezimmer. Das Erdgeschoss dient dem Wohnen, Speisen und Kunstgenuss.

Die Fassaden des Erd- und Obergeschosses sind mit einer schwarz lasierten, horizontalen Holzlattung verkleidet, die an traditionelle japanische Architektur erinnert. Sie ruhen über einem Sockel aus Sichtbeton, auf dem die sägerauhen Schalbretter ein ebenfalls horizontales Muster hinterlassen haben. So wirkt die Villa wie eine dunkle Holzbox auf einem Sockel, der nach Norden zur Hälfte im Hang steht. Im Obergeschoss öffnen große Bandfenster, im Sockel französische

French windows in the base open up the building to the outside. The garage has been neatly integrated into the building.

Residents and visitors enter the villa from the middle level that houses the kitchen as well as a double-floor living space with a fully glazed front wall. Its center is defined by a large cube with comfortable seating furniture and a gas fireplace, providing a retreat between the inside and the outside. The other built-in furniture items and the design of the garden also resonate with the minimalist architecture of the villa. The staircase, elegantly fixed only on one side, is naturally lit by a skylight. The non-structural partition walls are clad with stained dark multiplex board and have a timber-frame structure. The free-flowing spaces of the villa create a sense of comfort, being low-key yet elegant.

In ecological terms also, the building is exemplary without boasting about its sophistication. Ecological building design begins with wisely orienting the building and its different spaces: the Bauer-Raffaelli House and its large living spaces open up towards the valley in the south while it is almost completely shut off towards the

sol. Le garage est intégré discrètement à la maison.

On pénètre dans la villa au niveau intermédiaire, qui comprend la cuisine et un espace de séjour sur deux niveaux, entièrement vitré sur une de ses faces. Au centre, un grand cube, avec des sièges confortables et une cheminée au gaz, offre un lieu de repli entre l'intérieur et l'extérieur. Le reste du mobilier intégré – petite échelle – tout comme l'aménagement du jardin – grande échelle – s'inspirent également de l'architecture minimaliste de la villa. L'escalier élégant, encastré sur un seul côté, bénéficie d'un éclairage zénithal. Les cloisons sont à ossature bois avec parements en contreplaqué multiplis teinté de couleur sombre.

La fluidité de l'agencement produit une générosité plaisante et une élégance simple, sans étalage. La maison est également un modèle de construction écologique, sans que les concepts progressistes appliqués ne s'affichent de manière tapageuse. La construction écologique commence par l'orientation judicieuse de la maison et de la distribution intérieure. La Maison Bauer-Raffaelli s'ouvre au sud, en direction de la vallée et du soleil, avec ses grandes pièces

Fenster das Gebäude nach außen. Die Garage ist diskret in das Haus integriert.

Man betritt die Villa auf der Mittelebene, die neben dem Küchenkorpus einen zweigeschossigen Wohnraum mit einer vollständig verglasten Stirnwand aufnimmt. Sein Zentrum ist ein großer Kubus mit bequemen Sitzmöbeln und Gaskamin, der eine Rückzugszone zwischen innen und außen bietet. Auch die anderen Einbaumöbel im Kleinen ebenso wie die Gartengestaltung im Großen greifen die minimalistische Architektur der Villa auf. Der Treppenraum mit einer eleganten, einseitig eingespannten Treppe ist durch ein Oberlicht natürlich beleuchtet. Die nicht tragenden, lediglich raumdefinierenden Wände sind mit dunkel gebeizten Multiplexplatten beplankt und wurden in Holzständerbauweise errichtet. Die fließenden Räume der Villa erzeugen eine angenehme Großzügigkeit und eine unaufgeregte Eleganz, die nie auftrumpft.

Auch ökologisch ist das Wohnhaus vorbildlich, ohne dass die progressiven Konzepte marktschreierisch nach außen getragen würden. Ökologisches Bauen beginnt bei der sinnvollen Orientierung des Hauses und der Nutzungen darin: Das Haus Bauer-Raffaelli

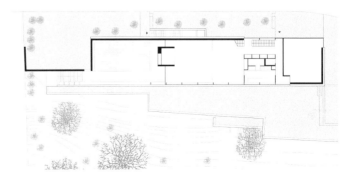

sunless north side and the street. The build-ing is heated by concrete core activation: a delicate network of pipes channels warm water into the concrete ceilings while so-lar collectors on the roof support the heat-ing and hot water system. The ventilation plant has a heat recovery system to make the best out of the applied energy. Before entering the house, the air is led through a thirty-meter-long pipe system located three meters below the ground. This ensures that the air can be naturally preheated in win-

de séjour. Côté nord, sans soleil, côté route, donc, elle est au contraire presque entière-ment fermée. La maison est chauffée par circulation d'eau chaude dans un réseau de tubes noyés dans les planchers intermédiai-res en béton. Des capteurs solaires en toi-ture servent d'appoint à la production d'eau chaude et au chauffage. L'installation de ven-tilation est équipée d'un système de récu-pération de chaleur afin de rentabiliser au maximum l'énergie consommée. Un puits canadien, constitué d'une canalisation de

öffnet sich mit seinen großen Wohnräumen zum Tal nach Süden und ist zur sonnenabge-wandten Nordseite und damit zur Straße hin fast vollständig geschlossen. Geheizt wird das Haus über eine Betonkernaktivierung: Warmes Wasser wird durch ein feines Rohr-leitungssystem in den Beton-Geschossde-cken geführt. Sonnenkollektoren auf dem Dach unterstützen die Warmwasseranlage sowie die Heizung. Die Lüftungsanlage hat eine Wärmerückgewinnungsanlage, um den besten Nutzen aus der eingesetzten Ener-

ter and pre-cooled in summer. Rain water is collected in an underground cistern next to the house and is used as gray water for the bathrooms. As such, the Bauer-Raffaelli House is at the cutting edge of environmental technology.

30 mètres de long, à trois mètres de profondeur, permet, de la manière la plus naturelle qui soit, de préchauffer l'air neuf en hiver et de le rafraîchir en été avant qu'il ne pénètre dans la maison. Les eaux de pluie sont récupérées dans une citerne enterrée, à côté de la maison, et utilisées pour les sanitaires. La maison Bauer-Raffaelli est bien à la pointe des techniques environnementales.

gie zu ziehen. Die Luft wird, bevor sie in das Haus gelangt, über ein 30 Meter langes, drei Meter tief unter der Erdoberfläche liegendes Rohrleitungssystem geführt, das im Winter die Luft auf natürliche Weise vorwärmen und sie im Sommer ebenso natürlich vorkühlen kann. Das Regenwasser wird in einer unterirdischen Zisterne neben dem Haus gesammelt und als Grauwasser für die Sanitärräume verwendet. Somit ist das Haus Bauer-Raffaelli auf dem neuesten Stand der Umwelttechnik.

RESIDENTIAL BUILDINGS IN HEISDORF (L)

IMMEUBLES D'HABITATION À HEISDORF (L)
WOHNUNGSBAU IN HEISDORF (L)

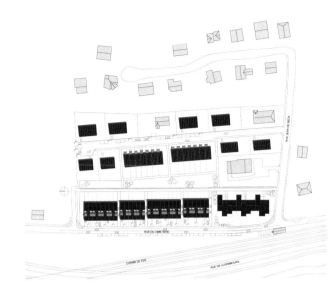

Heisdorf is a typical place close to the city limits of Luxembourg. It has rapidly grown in the last few years but has arguably not gained much in terms of an appropriate urban form. The new residential building project in the municipality of Steinsel had the objective of providing cost-effective residential space while also making an effort to more clearly define the spatial limits of the place. The housing scheme is based on a land development plan that envisages higher densities than have normally been applied in the small towns of Luxembourg. The long rectangular plot provides space for twenty-eight row houses that have been divided into four groups of between six and eight houses each. The rows follow the course of the topographical undulations along the street. The houses are comparatively compact but spacious enough to fill out the depth of the terrain. Covered atriums have been designed for all houses, channeling daylight into the interiors. Making skillful use of the topography, each house has a protected parking space at street level. The upper level, the garden floor, houses the kitchen and living spaces.

Heisdorf est une localité luxembourgeoise typique, proche de la capitale. Elle a connu une croissance rapide au cours des dernières années, sans nécessairement gagner en forme urbaine. Le nouveau projet immobilier réalisé pour le compte de la commune de Steinsel visait à la fois à proposer des habitations économiques et à tracer plus clairement les contours du bourg. L'ensemble s'appuie sur un plan d'aménagement urbain prévoyant un coefficient d'occupation des sols supérieur à ce qui est usuel par ailleurs pour les petites bourgades du Luxembourg.

Le terrain, un rectangle étiré dans la longueur, offrait l'espace nécessaire pour implanter 28 maisons en bandes, regroupées en quatre ensembles de six ou huit maisons chacun, échelonnés dans la légère pente le long de la rue. Les maisons sont relativement compactes mais suffisamment profondes pour occuper le terrain sur toute sa largeur. Elles possèdent toutes un atrium couvert qui assure un éclairage naturel jusqu'au cœur des maisons. Utilisant habilement la topographie de l'endroit, chacune d'elles dispose d'un emplacement de stationnement abrité au

Heisdorf ist ein typischer Ort nahe der Stadtgrenze Luxemburgs, der in den letzten Jahren schnell gewachsen ist, dabei aber nicht unbedingt an städtebaulicher Form gewonnen hat. Ziel des neuen Wohnungsbauprojekts für die Gemeinde Steinsel war es, kostengünstigen Wohnraum zu schaffen und gleichzeitig den Ortsrand klarer zu definieren. Die Siedlung basiert auf einem Bebauungsplan, der eine höhere Dichte vorsieht, als sonst in den Kleinstädten in Luxemburg üblich.

Die langgestreckte, rechteckige Parzelle bietet Raum für 28 Reihenhäuser, die in vier gestaffelten Gruppen mit je sechs bzw. acht Häusern zusammengefasst wurden. Die Reihen folgen dem leichten Höhenunterschied entlang der Straße. Die Häuser sind vergleichsweise kompakt, aber ausgedehnt genug, um die Tiefe des Terrains zu besetzen und verfügen alle über gedeckte Atrien, die natürliches Licht in die Tiefe des Hauses bringen. Die Topografie geschickt ausnutzend, hat jedes Haus einen geschützten Stellplatz im Geschoss auf Straßenniveau. Die darüberliegende Etage, das Gartengeschoss, beherbergt Küche und Wohnräume.

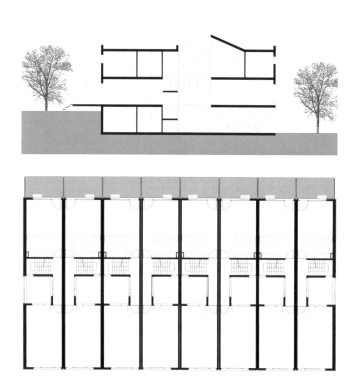

The colors of the wood-clad façades alternate between oxblood red and bluish gray while the fenestration varies from house to house following a certain predefined pattern that has four modules. The large windows admit a lot of daylight into the interiors and relate to the external spaces. Green roofs provide spectacular views, even for those living in the houses that date from the more recent building phases, further up the slope.

The Heisdorf project is intended to serve as proof that the advantages of (sub)urban living can be enjoyed even in a spatially tightly ordered layout, with subsidized owner-occupied houses at the city's edge, if they are sensitively designed. The row houses may be repetitive but are, in no way, monotonous.

niveau de la rue. Le niveau supérieur, qui est celui du jardin, accueille la cuisine et les pièces d'habitation.

Les couleurs du bardage en bois alternent entre un rouge brique et un gris bleuté. Le fenêtrage varie selon les maisons, avec quatre motifs différents. Les fenêtres, de grandes dimensions, offrent une luminosité importante et une proximité avec l'espace extérieur. Les futurs habitants des maisons des autres lots, plus haut dans la pente, jouissent d'une vue agréable sur les toitures-terrasses végétalisées.

Le projet de Heisdorf démontre ainsi qu'un ensemble de logements en copropriété subventionnés situé hors de la ville, avec des contraintes d'implantation, peut, s'il est soigneusement conçu, bénéficier des mêmes avantages que l'habitat urbain ou suburbain classique. Les maisons en bande sont certes répétitives mais n'ont pour autant rien de monotone.

Die Farben der holzverschalten Fassaden wechseln zwischen ochsenblutrot und blaugrau, die Befensterung variiert von Haus zu Haus innerhalb eines vorgegebenen Musters mit vier Modulen. Die großen Fenster lassen viel natürliches Licht in die Innenräume und stellen Bezüge zum Außenraum her. Extensiv begrünte Flachdächer garantieren auch den Bewohnern späterer Bauabschnitte der Siedlung weiter oben am Hang einen attraktiven Ausblick.

Das Projekt Heisdorf beweist, dass die Vorzüge (sub-)urbanen Wohnens bei sorgfältiger Gestaltung auch in einer räumlich geordneten Anlage mit geförderten Eigentumswohnungen am Stadtrand möglich sind. Die Reihenhäuser sind zwar repetitiv, aber keineswegs monoton gestaltet.

POOS HOUSE, SENNINGERBERG (L)

MAISON POOS, SENNINGERBERG (L)
HAUS POOS, SENNINGERBERG (L)

The white villa on the Senningerberg in Luxembourg was one of Christian Bauer's first projects in 1978. Following a change of ownership, an extensive renovation that included the outlying structures was undertaken in 2009.

The villa lies on a slope, delicately embedded into a small pinewood forest, which hides it from view. The slender pine trees filter the incoming daylight which enters the villa through large bay windows, creating a uniquely calm atmosphere. The steeply sloping terrain is the reason behind the three-storey spatial arrangement. At the side facing the street, the house has a single floor while on the garden side it has two more floors. A combination of round and

La villa blanche construite en 1978, dans le quartier du Senningerberg, à Luxembourg, avait été l'un des tous premiers projets de Christian Bauer. En 2009, après l'acquisition par de nouveaux propriétaires, elle a fait l'objet d'une importante rénovation, tandis que les espaces extérieurs étaient réaménagés.

La villa, située dans une pente, est si intelligemment insérée dans un petit bois de pins qu'on ne peut jamais la voir en totalité. Les pins, élancés, tamisent la lumière du jour qui pénètre à l'intérieur de la villa par de monumentaux bow-windows, créant une ambiance calme toute particulière. La déclivité importante du terrain explique la disposition en plan sur trois étages. Côté rue, la villa ne présente ainsi qu'un seul niveau,

Die weiße Villa am Senningerberg in Luxemburg von 1978 ist eines der ersten Projekte von Christian Bauer. 2009 wurde sie nach einem Besitzerwechsel umfassend renoviert, auch die Außenanlagen wurden neu gestaltet.

Die Villa liegt an einem Hang und ist so sensibel in ein kleines Kiefernwäldchen eingepasst, dass man sie nie vollständig sehen kann. Die schlanken Kiefern filtern das Tageslicht, das in die großen Erkerfenster der Villa fällt, und schaffen eine eigentümlich ruhige Atmosphäre. Das stark abfallende Gelände erklärt das Arrangement der Grundrisse über drei Etagen. Zur Straßenseite hin präsentiert sich das Haus einstöckig, zur Gartenseite hin jedoch hat es zwei weitere Etagen. Eine

straight shapes makes up the geometry of the house. The ground plan is reminiscent of a cloverleaf with three leaves. The living spaces are characterized by three large bay windows with a free-standing fireplace in the middle. Wonderful views of the valley's lush vegetation can be enjoyed from the living and dining room as well as from the library. The kitchen and an office are directly adjacent to the living spaces that are sunk three or four steps. The lowest floor houses the bed- and guest rooms. The middle floor is reserved for the children. An elegant spiral staircase connects the different levels with each other. While the space allocation has been arrived at rationally, the orientation towards the landscape, the sun and the topography have also played a major part. Even the furniture harmonizes with the relaxed, flowing architecture and its round, octagonal and trapezoidal spaces.

auquel s'en ajoutent deux autres côté jardin. Le volume combine formes arrondies et formes droites. Le plan est organisé comme un trèfle à trois feuilles. Le séjour est commandé par trois bow-windows avec, dans l'axe, une cheminée, dégagée de toutes parts. De la salle à manger – salle de séjour et de la bibliothèque, la vue ne peut faire autrement que de se perdre dans la magnifique végétation de la vallée. La cuisine et un bureau sont accolés aux pièces de séjour, en contrebas de trois ou quatre marches. Le niveau inférieur accueille les chambres à coucher et chambres d'amis. L'étage intermédiaire est réservé aux enfants, les différents niveaux étant reliés entre eux par un élégant escalier à vis. La distribution des pièces, rationnelle, tient compte de l'orientation par rapport au paysage, au soleil et à la topographie. Le mobilier lui-même est en harmonie avec l'architecture dégagée, souple, avec ses pièces de forme circulaire, octogonale ou trapézoïdale.

Kombination runder und gerader Formen bildet das Volumen des Hauses. Der Grundriss ist wie ein dreiblättriges Kleeblatt organisiert. Der Wohnraum wird von drei großen Erkerfenstern bestimmt, in deren Mitte ein Kamin frei im Raum steht. Vom Wohn- und Esszimmer und der Bibliothek fällt der Blick immer wieder in die herrliche Vegetation des Tals. Die Küche und ein Büro grenzen direkt an die Wohnräume, die drei oder vier Stufen abgesenkt liegen. Die unterste Etage nimmt die Schlaf- und Gästezimmer auf. Der mittlere Stock ist den Kindern vorbehalten. Eine elegante Wendeltreppe verbindet die Etagen miteinander. Die Raumaufteilung des Hauses ist rational, aber im Hinblick auf die Orientierung zur Landschaft, Sonne und Topografie hin konzipiert. Selbst die Möblierung steht im Einklang mit der legeren, fließenden Architektur und ihren runden, oktogonalen und trapezförmigen Räumen.

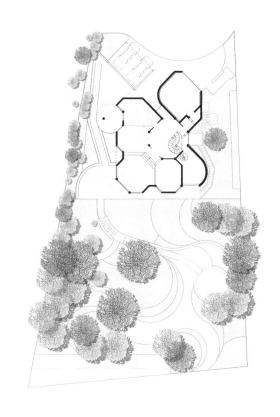

THE REPRESENTATION OF LUXEMBOURG AT THE EXPO 2000 IN HANOVER (D)

PRÉSENTATION DE LUXEMBOURG À L'EXPO 2000 À HANOVRE (D)

AUFTRITT LUXEMBURGS AUF DER EXPO 2000 IN HANNOVER (D)

Luxembourg had decided not to build its own pavilion at the Expo 2000 in Hanover but rather rent a display area in an existing exhibition hall. The architectural challenge was how to attract visually satiated visitors of the world exposition to the country's display. The architects succeeded in doing so by installing a large 3D cinema theater with a light-transmitting backlit glass façade that instantly became an attraction in the dark exhibition hall, symbolizing a welcoming gesture instead of a barrier. The glazed wall, ellipsoidal in plan, was gently inclined to one side.

Luxembourg's display was to a large extent supported by the satellite operator SES-ASTRA, one of the most important companies in the country. For this reason, information technology and telecommunications formed a particular focus. Visitors were shown a short 3D film on Luxembourg's position regarding worldwide issues and problems of contemporary relevance. A large free-standing wooden staircase led visitors back

Pour l'exposition universelle de Hanovre, Expo 2000, le Luxembourg avait décidé de ne pas construire de pavillon mais de louer un espace dans un hall existant. De ce fait, le défi architectural résidait dans la nécessité d'attirer et d'entretenir l'attention de visiteurs potentiels déjà sollicités à l'extrême par ailleurs. Les architectes y sont parvenus en utilisant une grande salle de cinéma 3D, avec une façade en verre translucide, éclairée de l'intérieur, qui captait le regard et constituait un pôle d'attraction lumineux dans le hall par ailleurs sombre – une invite balayant toute intimidation. La paroi en verre dessinait les contours d'un tronc de cône inversé, plan elliptique et parois légèrement inclinées.

Cette mise en scène du Luxembourg ayant été largement financée par l'opérateur de satellites SES-ASTRA, une des entreprises les plus importantes du Luxembourg, il était logique que l'informatique et les télécommunications soient particulièrement mises en valeur. Les visiteurs visionnaient un court film en 3D sur le Grand-Duché de Luxem-

Luxemburg hatte sich entschlossen, auf der Weltausstellung EXPO 2000 in Hannover keinen eigenen Pavillon zu bauen, sondern eine Fläche in einer bestehenden Messehalle zu mieten. Die architektonische Herausforderung bestand darin, die Aufmerksamkeit der reizüberfluteten Besucher der Weltausstellung anzuziehen und zu halten. Den Architekten gelang dies, indem sie einen großen 3-D-Kinosaal mit einer lichtdurchlässigen, hinterleuchteten Glasfassade zum Blickfang in der dunklen Halle machten – eine einladende Geste anstelle einer Hemmschwelle. Die Glaswand, im Grundriss ellipsoid, war zusätzlich leicht geneigt.

Der Auftritt Luxemburgs wurde maßgeblich von dem Satellitenbetreiber SES-ASTRA, einem der wichtigsten Unternehmen in Luxemburg, gefördert. Deshalb wurde der Aspekt der Informationstechnik und Telekommunikation besonders hervorgehoben. Den Besuchern wurde ein kurzer Film in 3-D-Technik über Luxemburgs Position zu weltweiten Phänomenen und Problemen

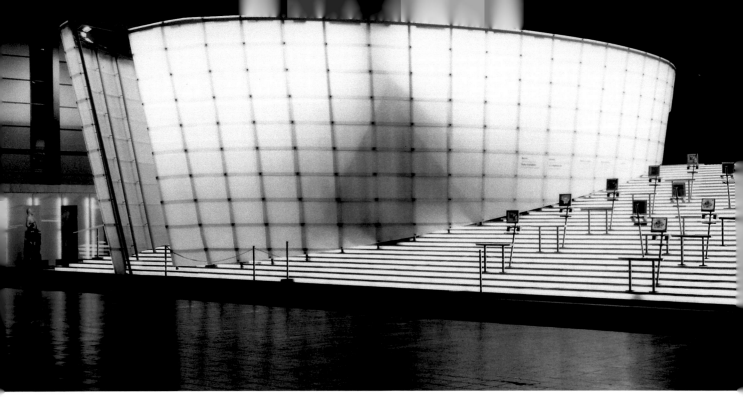

The Representation of Luxembourg at the Expo 2000 in Hanover (D) 52,3205° 9,8091°

to the corridor of the exhibition hall. The series of monitors that lined the staircase provided places to rest and an opportunity to obtain further information on the discussed issues online. Since the visibility of flat display stalls is rather limited in large exhibition halls, the staircase's inclined surface with its distinctive three-dimensional shape was a welcome idea.

bourg et ses orientations politiques et sociales. Ils pouvaient ressortir en redescendant dans le couloir du hall d'exposition par de très vastes degrés en bois. Si vastes qu'ils permettaient d'y aligner des postes informatiques – pour un approfondissement en ligne d'un sujet –, et aussi de s'asseoir. Les stands installés dans les halls d'exposition, au ras du sol, souffrent généralement d'un manque de visibilité. Ce n'était pas le cas ici, avec le plan incliné formé par ces degrés, qui offrait au contraire une troisième dimension et se faisait signal.

unserer Zeit gezeigt. Über eine große hölzerne Freitreppe gelangten sie wieder in den Gang der Messehalle. Die aufgereihten Monitore auf der Treppe boten neben Sitzgelegenheiten die Möglichkeit, online vertiefende Informationen einzuholen. Da in Messehallen bei flachen Ausstellungsständen die Sichtbarkeit meist leidet, bot die „gekippte Fläche" der Treppe auch eine markante dreidimensionale Form.

OFFICE BUILDING ON RUE STÜMPER, LUXEMBOURG (L)

IMMEUBLE DE BUREAUX RUE STÜMPER, LUXEMBOURG (L)
BÜROHAUS RUE STÜMPER, LUXEMBURG (L)

Over the last few years, a new commercial and industrial district has come up on a site that formerly housed a printing press along the Rue Stümper in Luxembourg. Like many such sites in the country, there regrettably is no higher urban planning structure in place. The office building at No. 7 Rue Stümper therefore attempts to define a "building with character," using a simple shape that would bring a sense of calmness into the motley architecture of the neighborhood.

A vertical façade with louvers faces the street on the western side, providing visual and glare protection while also helping in reducing the cooling requirement of the building in summer. The louvers are divided into movable segments. Their glass surfaces have different patterns made up of colorful dots in five different tones of green and gray. The windows behind have shutters that can be partly opened.

Since the office building was designed without knowing who the users would be, the architecture has been devised to be flexible without appearing too neutral or drab.

Une zone de bureaux et d'activité s'est implantée au cours de ces dernières années sur le terrain d'une ancienne imprimerie, le long de la rue Stümper à Luxembourg. Comme beaucoup de zones de ce type au Luxembourg, elle fait douloureusement regretter un projet d'ensemble. Le bâtiment de bureaux au n°7 de la rue est, de ce fait, un bâtiment « de caractère » mais de forme simple, qui tente d'apporter un peu d'apaisement dans un voisinage disparate agité.

Côté rue, la façade orientée ouest est habillée de lames verticales qui servent aussi bien de pare-vue que de pare-soleil, limitant en été les besoins en climatisation. Ces lames en verre sont découpées en segments mobiles indépendants les uns des autres. Elles s'ornent de motifs sérigraphiés différents, constitués de points de couleur, dans cinq tons de gris et de vert. À l'abri de ces lames, la façade comporte des ouvrants.

S'agissant d'un immeuble en blanc – dont les utilisateurs sont inconnus au stade du projet –, l'architecture s'efforce d'être flexible sans pour autant tomber dans la neutralité.

Auf einem ehemaligen Druckereigelände entlang der Rue Stümper in Luxemburg ist in den letzten Jahren ein Büro- und Gewerbegebiet entstanden, das – wie viele solcher Areale in Luxemburg – eine übergeordnete städtebauliche Planung schmerzlich vermissen lässt. Das Bürohaus in der Rue Stümper Nr. 7 versucht deshalb, als „Gebäude mit Charakter" mit einer einfachen Form ein wenig Ruhe in die aufgeregte, kunterbunte Nachbarschaft zu bringen.

Das Gebäude zeigt sich mit einer vertikalen Lamellenfassade nach Westen zur Straße hin, die sowohl Sicht- und Blendschutz bietet als auch hilft, den Kühlbedarf des Hauses im Sommer zu reduzieren. Die Lamellen sind in Segmenten beweglich gestaltet; ihre Glasflächen haben unterschiedliche Muster aus Farbpunkten in fünf verschiedenen Grün- und Grautönen. Die dahinterliegenden Fenster haben teilweise Öffnungsflügel.

Da es sich um ein spekulatives Bürohaus handelt, bei dem während des Entwurfs die Nutzer noch nicht feststehen, strebt die Architektur danach, flexibel zu sein, ohne

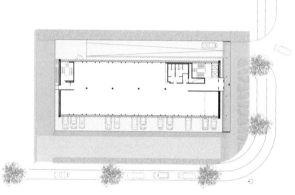

Having only one row of columns, and a convenient ratio of gross area to net area, the design follows strict economic parameters. The four office levels rest on stilts, floating above a trough that provides space for parking without having to be artificially lighted or ventilated. The entrance façade is clad with zinc plate modules while a sculpture of light adorns the stair well.

Avec une seule file de poteaux et un rapport favorable entre surface hors œuvre brute et surface hors œuvre nette, le projet satisfait des critères économiques stricts. Les quatre niveaux de bureaux s'élèvent au-dessus d'une trémie offrant un espace de parking qui ne nécessite ni éclairage artificiel ni ventilation. Côté entrée, le pignon, habillé de cassettes en tôles de zinc, est animé par un grand portique décoratif. Une sculpture de lumière décore le jour de l'escalier.

dabei neutral zu werden. Mit nur einer Stützenreihe und einem günstigen Verhältnis von Brutto- zu Nettofläche folgt der Entwurf strengen wirtschaftlichen Vorgaben. Die vier Büroetagen sind über einem Trog aufgeständert, der Parkraum bietet, ohne künstlich belichtet oder belüftet werden zu müssen. Die Eingangsfassade ist mit Zinkblechkassetten gestaltet, eine Lichtskulptur schmückt das Treppenauge.

SENIOR CITIZEN'S RESIDENCE, STRASSEN (L)

RÉSIDENCE POUR PERSONNES ÂGÉES, STRASSEN (L)
ALTENGERECHTES WOHNEN, STRASSEN (L)

In the winter of their lives, many people feel the need to live in a community that simultaneously offers them adequate space to express their individuality. In architectural terms, the objective was to avoid the potentially oppressive atmosphere of a senior citizens' home and to create comfortable surroundings while fulfilling all functional requirements.

The architects split the space allocation requirements into two buildings: a residential building with a large centrally-placed atrium and a day-care center. A pergola with a glass roof connects the two parts. The single-story day-care center has an elongated ground plan, with a box-like space housing side rooms dividing it into a dining and a meeting hall. A long covered terrace along the entire length of the building allows for views into the garden.

The façades extend along both buildings. For the day-care center and the plinth of the residential building, slate panels have been used.

The large atrium of the main building is the social heart of the complex and doubles as a lounge. On both sides of the atrium, ar-

Avec l'âge, beaucoup de personnes ont besoin d'habiter en communauté, mais une communauté qui réserve un espace d'individualité. Le point de départ du projet architectural de la résidence pour personnes âgées de Strassen était d'éviter le caractère de maison de retraite : agrément et fonctionnalité ne devaient pas être exclusifs l'un de l'autre.

Les architectes ont distribué les fonctions du programme entre un bâtiment d'habitation d'une part et un centre de jour d'autre part, reliés entre eux par un passage couvert d'une verrière. Le centre de jour, sur un seul niveau, est un bâtiment allongé – avec salle à manger et salle de séjour –, divisé en deux par un noyau accueillant les locaux de service. Il est doublé, sur toute sa longueur, par une terrasse couverte avec vue sur le jardin. Les façades créent une unité entre les deux bâtiments : un parement en béton, avec inclusions d'éléments en schiste, a été retenu à la fois pour le centre de jour et pour le soubassement du bâtiment résidentiel. Celui-ci comporte un grand atrium, où bat le cœur de la résidence, et qui sert largement d'espace de séjour. On accède aux apparte-

Im Alter haben viele Menschen das Bedürfnis, in einer Gemeinschaft zu wohnen, die dennoch Raum für Individualität lässt. Architektonisch war der Ausgangspunkt beim Entwurf des altengerechten Wohnhauses in Strassen die Vermeidung eines „Anstalts-Charakters": Eine wohnliche Umgebung und die funktionalen Anforderungen sollten sich nicht ausschließen.

Die Architekten haben das Programm in zwei Gebäude aufgeteilt: ein Wohnhaus mit großem Atrium in der Mitte und eine Tagesstätte. Eine Pergola mit Glasdach verbindet beide Teile. Die eingeschossige Tagesstätte hat einen langgestreckten Grundriss und ist durch eine eingestellte Box mit Nebenräumen in einen Speise- und einen Veranstaltungssaal unterteilt. Über die ganze Länge bietet eine lange, überdeckte Terrasse den Blick in den Garten.

Die Fassaden fassen beide Gebäude zusammen. Für die Tagesstätte und den Sockel des Wohngebäudes wurden Schieferpaneele gewählt.

Das große Atrium des Hauptgebäudes fungiert als soziales Herz der Anlage und Aufenthaltsraum. Auf beiden Seiten des

cades that are undulating on one side and straight on the other, connect the single and double room apartments with each other. The swaying arcades not only enliven the atrium space, they also create an environment where one can "see and be seen". Daylight reaches the atrium through a long skylight. Photovoltaic modules are integrated into every second glass roof panel. These

ments, avec chambres simples ou doubles, par des coursives sur chaque côté. Sur l'un, elles ont un contour onduleux, sur l'autre le contour est droit. Les courbes des coursives n'ont pas seulement un effet visuel d'animation, elles créent aussi des espaces d'où l'on peut « voir et être vu ».
Une longue ouverture assure un éclairage zénithal de l'atrium, en alternant panneaux

Atriums erschließen Laubengänge – auf der einen Seite geschwungen, auf der anderen gerade – die Wohnungen mit Einzel- und Doppelzimmern. Die Ausbuchtungen der Laubengänge beleben nicht nur visuell den Raum des Atriums, sie schaffen auch Plätze für das „Sehen und Gesehenwerden". Tageslicht dringt von oben durch ein langes Oberlicht in das Atrium. In jedem zweiten

also shade the courtyard in summer and prevent it from overheating. All apartments have small windows facing the atrium and large balconies on another side providing views of the locality and of a park.

simplement vitrés et panneaux vitrés à cellules photovoltaïques. L'ombre projetée par ces derniers en été protège la cour intérieure d'un échauffement excessif. Les appartements comportent tous de petites fenêtres donnant sur l'atrium et de grands balcons avec vue soit sur le village de Strassen, soit sur un parc, en fonction de l'orientation.

Feld befinden sich Photovoltaik-Module, die durch ihre verschattende Funktion den Innenhof im Sommer vor Überhitzung schützen. Alle Wohnungen haben kleine Fenster zum Atrium hin und auf der gegenüberliegenden Seite große Balkone mit Blick über das Örtchen auf der einen und einen Park auf der anderen Seite.

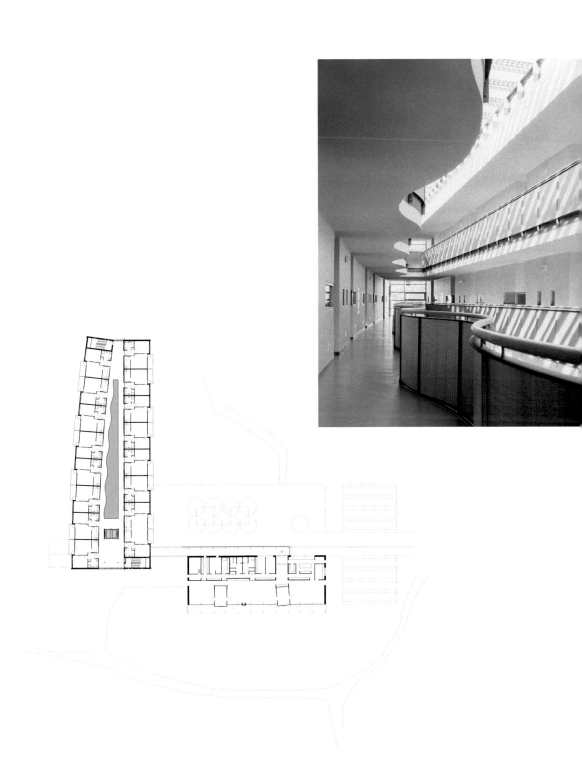

ADMINISTRATIVE BUILDING OF THE A+P KIEFFER OMNITEC COMPANY, LUXEMBOURG (L)

SIÈGE DE LA SOCIÉTÉ A+P KIEFFER OMNITEC, LUXEMBOURG (L)
VERWALTUNGSGEBÄUDE DER FIRMA A+P KIEFFER OMNITEC, LUXEMBURG (L)

When a sophisticated engineering company intends to build a new building for its administration, it expects not only the design of an architectural visiting card for itself but also the construction of an exemplary climate-conscious building. The administrative building of the a+p kieffer omnitec company is located in the industrial area of Cloche d'Or in Luxembourg City, impressively demonstrating how appealing contemporary architecture and sensitive energy-saving building techniques are able to support each other. The approximately 5,000-square-meter-large building is fitted with a heating system of a size that would normally be installed for a much smaller apartment building.

The four office floors are located above an open parking level that replaces an expensive and lavish underground parking lot, with a workshop next to it. The narrow building faces the south. Clad in larch wood panels that weather differently due to their changing alignment, the façade creates a lively overall image. The walls surrounding the sunken courtyard are covered with vines and ivy plants and help create a natural micro-climate buffer around the building. Entrances are located along the front and rear façades of the building that has a central corridor running along its entire length. It is left without

Lorsqu'un constructeur d'installations de climatisation et de chauffage à la pointe du progrès fait faire un projet pour abriter son siège, l'architecture de son bâtiment doit non seulement constituer la carte de visite de la société, elle doit aussi montrer de quoi les concepts modernes de conditionnement d'air sont capables. C'est le cas pour le siège de la société a+p kieffer omnitec, installé à côté de ses ateliers, dans la zone d'activité de la Cloche d'Or, à Luxembourg. Il démontre brillamment comment une architecture contemporaine qui flatte la vue et des techniques de construction intelligentes et économes en énergie se renforcent mutuellement. Le bâtiment d'environ 5000 mètres carrés est chauffé avec une installation tout juste dimensionnée, normalement, pour du tout petit habitat collectif.

Les quatre étages de bureaux surmontent un parking ouvert, alternative à un parking souterrain complexe et coûteux. Le bâtiment, étroit parallélépipède, est entièrement orienté au sud. Les façades, revêtues d'un lattis de mélèze, sont animées par l'évolution inégale de celui-ci selon l'orientation et l'exposition à la pluie. Les murs qui cernent la cour inférieure, tapissés de vigne vierge et de lierre, contribuent à produire un espace tampon climatique naturel autour

Wenn ein progressiver Anlagenbauer für seine Verwaltung einen Neubau entwerfen lässt, soll dieser nicht nur architektonisch die Visitenkarte der Firma sein, sondern auch zeigen, was moderne Klimakonzepte leisten können. Das Verwaltungsgebäude der Firma a+p kieffer omnitec befindet sich im Gewerbegebiet Cloche d'Or in Luxemburg-Stadt und demonstriert eindrucksvoll, wie ansprechende zeitgenössische Architektur und sinnvolle, energiesparende Bauweisen einander befördern können: Das rund 5000 Quadratmeter große Haus wird mit einer Heizung versorgt, deren Bemessung normalerweise gerade einmal für ein Mehrfamilienhaus ausreichen würde.

Die vier Büroetagen liegen über einer offenen Parkebene, die eine teure und aufwendige Tiefgarage ersetzt. Daneben befindet sich eine Werkstatt. Der schmale Gebäuderiegel ist nach Süden orientiert. Die Fassaden sind mit Lärchenholzlatten verkleidet, die je nach Ausrichtung ungleichmäßig verwittern und damit ein lebendiges Bild ergeben. Die Wände, die den tiefer liegenden Hof umgeben, sind mit Wein und Efeu berankt und helfen, einen natürlichen Klimapuffer um das Haus zu erzeugen. Die Eingänge führen von den Schmalseiten ins Haus, das der Länge nach über einen Mit-

cladding so that its thermal mass can help in considerably reducing the requirement for heating in winter and cooling in summer. There are neither suspended ceilings nor double floors. The rooms have a spacious clearance height of 3.10 meters. The high windows allow daylight to reach deep into the space while retaining a massive balustrade to avoid the undesirable greenhouse effect that all-glass buildings tend to produce. In order to protect the spaces in summer from overheating, external sun-shading devices have been installed.

Both the roof and the façades have been insulated following the highest standards. Concrete core activation has been applied for the ceilings that are equipped with a ventilation system. The adiabatic air conditioning coupled with the nightly cooling of the concrete components meet the comfort

du bâtiment. Les entrées sont situées dans les pignons, un couloir central desservant chaque niveau dans le sens de la longueur. Il n'a reçu aucun habillage, afin que son inertie thermique puisse contribuer à une réduction sensible des besoins de chauffage en hiver et des besoins de rafraîchissement en été. Sans plafonds suspendus ni doubles planchers, les locaux ont une hauteur sous plafond généreuse de 3,10 mètres. Les hautes fenêtres laissent pénétrer profondément la lumière du jour, en dépit de la présence d'une allège en béton destinée à éviter l'effet de serre indésirable que l'on observe dans les bâtiments entièrement vitrés. Des stores extérieurs protègent les locaux d'une chaleur estivale excessive.

L'isolation de la toiture et des façades, qui satisfait les critères les plus stricts, est complétée par des plafonds rafraîchissants fonc-

telflur erschlossen wird. Er ist unverkleidet, damit seine thermische Masse dabei helfen kann, den Bedarf an Heizung im Winter und Kühlung im Sommer spürbar zu reduzieren. Es gibt weder abgehängte Decken noch Doppelböden. Die Räume haben eine großzügige lichte Höhe von 3,10 Metern. Die hohen Fenster lassen das Tageslicht bis tief in den Raum einfallen und haben dennoch eine massive Brüstung, um den unerwünschten Gewächshaus-Effekt von Ganzglasgebäuden zu vermeiden. Um die Räume im Sommer vor Überhitzung zu schützen, gibt es einen außen liegenden Sonnenschutz.

Dach und Fassaden sind auf höchstem Standard gedämmt und das Gebäude verfügt über eine Betonkernaktivierung der Decken, die mit einer Lüftungsanlage gekoppelt ist. Die adiabatische Kühlung in der Klimaanlage gepaart mit der Nachtauskühlung der

requirements during most of the summer. During times of excessively high humidity, a dehumidifying module lowers humidity levels in the air supply. The architecture of the a+p kieffer omnitec headquarters dispenses entirely with high-tech solutions.

tionnant sur le seul principe de l'inertie thermique, sans apport d'énergie, couplés à une installation de ventilation. Le refroidissement adiabatique de l'installation de climatisation, auquel s'ajoute le rafraîchissement nocturne des composants en béton, assure un confort satisfaisant pendant la plus grande partie de l'été. Lorsque le temps est particulièrement lourd, un déshumidificateur abaisse le taux d'hygrométrie de l'air neuf à un niveau adéquat. On le voit : l'architecture du siège de la société a+p kieffer omnitec se passe très bien de technologie de pointe.

Betonkomponenten genügt den Komfortansprüchen für die längste Zeit des Sommers. Bei extremer Schwüle bringt ein Entfeuchtermodul die nötige Absenkung des Feuchtegehalts in der Zuluft. Die Architektur des Hauptsitzes der Firma a+p kieffer omnitec kommt ganz ohne Hightech aus.

MONTEREY BUILDING, CENTRAL BANK, LUXEMBOURG (L)

BÂTIMENT MONTEREY, BANQUE CENTRALE, LUXEMBOURG (L)
GEBÄUDE MONTEREY, ZENTRALBANK, LUXEMBURG (L)

With the construction of the new Monterey building of the Central Bank of Luxembourg two conceptual and architectural objectives have been met: firstly, the building's integration into its urban context and secondly, the expression of the building's architectural individuality that underlines the image of the central bank. The building actually comprises two separate parts that stand in dialog with each other. The part built in stone, with its emblematic and staggered openings, faces the Avenue Monterey with its traffic and rather uninspiring view. The slanting shape of the building underlines its corner situation. The glass-clad building is the architects' answer to the park opposite. With its glass louvers, a double façade provides effective protection from the sun without restricting transparency.

The ground plan of the building is determined by two load-carrying cores that house the service spaces and give the office floors the required flexibility. A numismatic museum is located on the ground floor. The

Le concept architectural du bâtiment Monterey de la Banque centrale du Luxembourg se caractérise par deux ambitions *a priori* contradictoires : une intégration dans l'environnement urbain d'une part, une affirmation de l'objet architectural individuel d'autre part, celui-ci se démarquant de son environnement et soulignant par là son indépendance, à l'image de celle de la Banque centrale. Le bâtiment est constitué de deux corps qui dialoguent chacun avec leur vis-à-vis respectif. Le corps principal, en pierre, très graphique avec ses baies décalées, répond à l'avenue Monterey, avec son trafic et sa vue sans intérêt. Le contre-fruit donné à la façade accentue la situation d'angle. L'avant-corps en verre, lui, est la réponse au parc qui fait face, sur l'autre côté. La façade double, avec ses lames de verre, offre une protection solaire efficace, sans altérer la transparence.

Le plan du bâtiment est déterminé par deux noyaux porteurs dans lesquels sont logés les locaux de service et qui assurent aux

Zwei unterschiedliche Ansprüche prägen das architektonische Konzept des Gebäudes Monterey für die Zentralbank Luxemburg: Integration in das städtebauliche Umfeld und Eigenständigkeit des individuellen Architekturobjektes, das sich von seinem Umfeld absetzt und seine Unabhängigkeit und somit die der Zentralbank unterstreicht. Das Volumen des Gebäudes wird von zwei Baukörpern gebildet, die mit den Besonderheiten der verschiedenen Ausrichtungen im Dialog stehen. Der Baukörper aus Stein, mit seinen zeichenhaften, gegeneinander versetzten Öffnungen, antwortet auf die Avenue Monterey mit ihrem Verkehr und ihrer uninteressanten Aussicht. Das abgeschrägte Volumen akzentuiert die Ecksituation. Der Glaskörper ist die Antwort auf den gegenüberliegenden Park. Diese Doppelfassade mit ihren Glaslamellen bietet einen effektiven Sonnenschutz, ohne die Transparenz abzuschwächen.

Der Grundriss des Gebäudes ist bestimmt durch zwei tragende Kerne, die die Neben-

uppermost floor with its high ceiling areas houses a multipurpose hall. The adjacent reception areas can be converted into classrooms that are fully equipped with monitors by means of a folding mechanism. The most commonly used materials are natural stone and wood. Stone from the Bourgogne region has been chosen due to its expressive character and its wine-red veins. It is used both for the façade and as flooring material. The load-bearing cores are clad in oak wood and form a contrast to the red-colored elements that are distributed in the whole building, from the doors to the columns of the museum.

The entrance door has inserts of one-Euro coins of the countries belonging to the Euro zone, thus referring to the purpose of the building. The memory of the old building is kept alive by fragments of the earlier window frames made of sandstone that are integrated into the black concrete of the gabled façade. Both the building's micro-form, represented by the use of coins, as well as its macro-form, owing to its overall design, serve to integrate its geometrical coherence with the diversity of its materials.

plateaux de bureaux la flexibilité nécessaire. Le rez-de-chaussée abrite un musée numismatique. Au dernier étage, dans les espaces de grande hauteur, un auditorium a été aménagé. Les espaces de réception voisins sont transformables, par un mécanisme de basculement, en salles de cours avec écrans. Les principaux matériaux utilisés sont la pierre naturelle et le bois. La pierre de Bourgogne a été choisie pour son caractère affirmé, dû à ses veines lie de vin. Elle est utilisée à la fois en façade et en revêtement de sol. Les noyaux porteurs sont revêtus de chêne et contrastent avec les éléments laqués rouge que l'on retrouve dans tout le bâtiment, des portes jusqu'aux totems du musée.

La porte d'entrée a été dessinée avec des inclusions de pièces de 1 euro de tous les pays de la zone euro, évocation claire de la fonction du bâtiment. Le souvenir du bâtiment antérieur est conservé par des fragments des anciens encadrements de fenêtre en grès, intégrés au béton noir du pignon. Ainsi, de la microforme (monnaie) à la macroforme (volumétrie), l'objectif est d'affirmer l'identité du bâtiment.

räume aufnehmen und den Büroetagen die nötige Flexibilität ermöglichen. Im Erdgeschoss befindet sich ein numismatisches Museum. Im obersten Geschoss wurde in den Bereichen mit großer Raumhöhe ein Mehrzwecksaal eingerichtet. Die danebenliegenden Empfangsbereiche können durch einen Ausklappmechanismus in Lehrbereiche mit Monitoren umgewandelt werden. Die wichtigsten verwendeten Materialien sind Naturstein und Holz. Der Stein aus der Bourgogne ist aufgrund seines ausdrucksstarken Charakters, der durch die weinroten Adern hervorgerufen wird, ausgewählt worden. Er findet sowohl in der Fassade als auch als Bodenbelag Anwendung. Die tragenden Kerne sind mit Eichenholz verkleidet und bilden einen Kontrast zu den rot lackierten Elementen, die sich im ganzen Gebäude wiederfinden, von den Türen bis zu den Stelen des Museums.

Die Eingangstür ist mit Einschlüssen von 1-Euro-Münzen der Länder der Eurozone gestaltet und weist so auf die Aufgabe des Gebäudes hin. Die Erinnerung an das ehemalige Gebäude wird durch Fragmente der ehemaligen Fenstereinrahmungen aus Sandstein aufrechterhalten, die in den schwarzen Beton der Giebelfassade eingelassen sind. Ausgehend von der Mikroform (Geldstücke) bis zur Makroform (Volumetrie) ist es das Ziel, die geometrische Kohärenz mit der Verschiedenheit der Materialien zu vereinen.

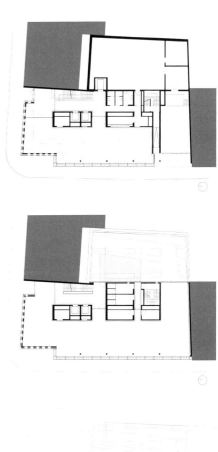

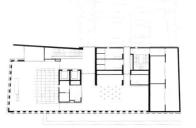

URBAN PLANNING

Urban Planning Competition Entry "Nordstad" (L), 2006 The six municipalities of Bettendorf, Colmar-Berg, Diekirch, Erpeldange, Ettelbruck, and Schieren are to be turned into an interconnected "capital of northern Luxembourg." This calls for the transformation of the heterogeneous elements into a separate urban body which can create a sense of identity and community. It also represents a rare opportunity for the planners, cba and Meurer Architekten to implement an urban planning approach that would create an entirely new urban entity imbibing the dynamic polarities between landscape and city, allowing for the combination of excellent open spaces with high urban densities. The topography and the landscape comprising the rivers Sauer and Alzette are envisaged to grow into a unified "cityscape," in keeping with the leitmotif of the "Nordstad" concept. Due to the large area under consideration, the definition of a central zone housing important facilities and the design of a new city entrance are an absolute necessity. A polycentric layout is, however, to be retained.

The "Nordstad" municipalities are compelled to strengthen their settlement structures,

Concours d'urbanisme pour la « Nordstad » (L), 2006 Les six communes de Bettendorf, Colmar-Berg, Diekirch, Erpeldange, Ettelbruck et Schieren ont vocation à se « souder », pour devenir la « capitale » du nord – la « Nordstad » – du Luxembourg. Cela impose un ordonnancement des constructions hétérogènes qui s'échelonnent entre les communes, de façon à créer une entité urbaine et résidentielle qui soit créatrice d'identité et de lien. L'équipe d'urbanistes cba et Meurer Architekten voit dans ce projet une opportunité rare d'appliquer un modèle d'urbanisme unifiant la polarité entre campagne et urbanité, en associant les qualités des espaces extérieurs à la densité urbaine. Selon leur proposition, la topographie et les espaces naturels de la Sûre et de l'Alzette doivent devenir un « paysage urbain » et l'emblème de la « Nordstad ». Compte tenu de l'étendue de cette nouvelle agglomération, l'aménagement d'une entrée de ville, la création d'un « cœur » et le regroupement de fonctions centrales constituent une condition *sine qua non* qui ne doit pas, pour autant, exclure la polycentralité.

Städtebaulicher Wetbewerb „Nordstad" (L), 2006 Die sechs Gemeinden Bettendorf, Colmar-Berg, Diekirch, Erpeldange, Ettelbruck und Schieren sollen zu einer zusammenhängenden „Hauptstadt des Nordens" von Luxemburg werden. Dafür bedarf es einer Ordnung der heterogenen Agglomerationen zwischen den Gemeinden hin zu einem Stadt- und Siedlungskörper, der Identität stiftet und Gemeinschaft fördert. Die Planer, cba und Meurer Architekten, sehen in dem Vorhaben die seltene Chance, ein städtebauliches Leitbild zu verfolgen, das aus der Polarität von Landschaft und Urbanität ein neues Ganzes erschafft und die freiräumlichen Qualitäten mit urbaner Dichte verbindet. Die Topografie, der Landschaftsraum der Flüsse Sauer und Alzette, soll – das ist das Leitbild der „Nordstad" – zu einer „Stadtlandschaft" werden. Wegen der Weiträumigkeit des Siedlungskörpers ist die Setzung eines zentralen Bereichs, einer Bündelung zentraler Funktionen und die Formulierung eines Stadteingangs eine Conditio sine qua non. Die Polyzentralität soll dennoch aufrechterhalten werden.

Die „Nordstad"-Gemeinden müssen ihre Siedlungsstrukturen stärken, die Kerne ver-

SAUER RIVER WALK IN ETTELBRÜCK

densify their centers, and clearly define urban limits vis-à-vis the non-urban landscape. Daily supplies, education, leisure, youth facilities, cultural events, and sports are to be locally provided. Simultaneously, central inter-municipal facilities are also envisaged. The "boulevard urbain," the central city axis between Ettelbruck and Diekirch is to be divided into sections by green belts. The allocated sites have defined plots where construction is permissible, thus making interconnected housing zones possible, which can, at the same time, be individually constructed. The transportation plan has the objective of reducing journey distances. Along the "boulevard urbain" mixed-use urban quarters are to be built. Living, working, and daily supply facilities as well as educational and care facilities are to be located in close proximity to each other. A "Nordstad" shuttle service using trams is to provide fast and efficient east-west connectivity.

The open space planning takes up the site's location at the river and the dynamic topography of the edges of the valley: diverse leisure facilities are to be built, while the city and the landscape, working and living re-

Les communes de la « Nordstad » doivent renforcer leur tissu urbain, densifier leurs centres et mieux dessiner leurs franges par rapport à la campagne environnante. Commerces de proximité, enseignement, loisirs, culture, sport, activités pour la jeunesse doivent être offerts localement. Mais il s'agit aussi de créer des lieux centraux, utilisés de manière intercommunale. Le Boulevard urbain, l'axe central entre Ettelbruck et Diekirch, est entrecoupé par des trouées vertes. La division en zones réservées à la construction permet d'envisager des quartiers d'un seul tenant pouvant être réalisés en tant que tels. Le schéma de circulation est celui d'une ville compacte et multifonctionnelle. Le Boulevard urbain aligne des quartiers mixtes combinant, côte à côte, logements, lieux de travail, commerces de proximité, établissements d'enseignement et crèches. Une navette (tramway) doit assurer une liaison est-ouest rapide.

L'aménagement des espaces extérieurs tire parti de la situation en bordure de rivière et de la topographie à flanc de vallée. Le projet prévoit une ville avec de nombreuses offres de loisirs et une interpénétration étroite de

dichten und ihre Siedlungsränder gegenüber der Landschaft betonen. Nahversorgung, Bildung, Freizeit, Jugend, Kultur und Sport müssen lokal bedient werden. Auf der anderen Seite sollen „interkommunal" genutzte, zentrale Stätten entstehen. Der „Boulevard urbain", die zentrale Stadtachse zwischen Ettelbruck und Diekirch, wird durch Grünschneisen in Abschnitte gegliedert. Die Teilung in Baufenster ermöglicht zusammenhängende Siedlungsbereiche, die als Einheiten realisiert werden können. Das Verkehrskonzept basiert auf der „Stadt der kurzen Wege". Entlang des „Boulevard urbain" sind Stadtquartiere mit Mischnutzungen vorgesehen; Wohnen, Arbeiten und Nahversorgung sowie Bildungs- und Betreuungseinrichtungen sollen sich Tür an Tür zueinander befinden. Ein Nordstad-Shuttle (Straßenbahn) soll für eine schnelle Ost-West-Verbindung sorgen.

Die Freiraumplanung greift die Lage am Fluss und die bewegte Topografie an den Talrändern auf: Geplant ist eine Stadt mit vielfältigen Freizeitangeboten sowie einer engen Durchdringung von Stadt und Landschaft, Wohnen und Arbeiten. Am Fluss

AERIAL VIEW OF THE CENTRAL CITY AXIS | VIEW FROM THE SAUER RIVER VALLEY TO THE TRIANGLE ERPELDANGE-LADUNO

quirements, flow into each other. Parks that harmonize with the landscape will be laid out by the river, while the green belts will provide urban parks. What makes the concept unique is the project's ambitious objective to offer high-quality urban living within a unique landscape, combined with excellent infrastructure facilities. The concept is based on ameliorating the quality of life by enabling urban living in harmony with nature, while also offering good employment opportunities and time savings due to outstanding transportation links.

Master Plan for Dudelange Schmelz (L), 2009 With its 18,000 inhabitants, Dudelange is Luxembourg's third largest city and, together with Esch-sur-Alzette, the most important industrial location of the country. A recently held competition had the objective of drawing up a master plan for Dudelange that would densify the urban quarters of "Schmelz" and "Italy" and sensitively link them to the existing architecture.

Cba, together with Latz und Partner and R+T verkehrsplaner, proposed a network of streets inspired by the orthogonal structure

la ville et de la campagne, de l'habitat et de l'activité. Le long de la Sûre, il est prévu la création de parcs de caractère naturel, dans les trouées vertes entrecoupant l'axe, des parcs de type urbain. Pouvoir offrir ainsi des logements qui bénéficient à la fois d'une grande qualité urbaine, d'un paysage unique et d'infrastructures performantes est exceptionnel. La qualité de vie, obtenue par un habitat proche de la nature au cœur de la ville, de bons postes de travail et des gains de temps du fait de dessertes remarquables, est à la base-même du projet.

Masterplan de Dudelange-Schmelz (L), 2009 Dudelange est, avec ses 18 000 habitants, la troisième plus grande ville du Luxembourg et, avec Esch-sur-Alzette, le pôle industriel le plus important du pays. Le concours d'urbanisme de Dudelange avait pour objectif une densification urbaine sur les friches industrielles entre les quartiers « Schmelz » et « Italie », et celle-ci devait être en ligne avec les principes du développement durable et se marier astucieusement aux constructions existantes.

Cba, en association avec Latz und Partner

sollen naturnahe, in den Grünschneisen urbane Parks entstehen. Das Potenzial, Wohnen in höchster städtischer Qualität mit einmaliger Landschaft und einer guten Infrastruktur zu verbinden, ist außergewöhnlich. Das Konzept basiert auf Lebensqualität durch naturnahes Wohnen in der Stadt, gute Arbeitsplätze und Zeitersparnis aufgrund einer hervorragenden Verkehrsanbindung.

Masterplan Dudelange-Schmelz (L), 2009 Dudelange ist mit 18.000 Einwohnern die drittgrößte Stadt Luxemburgs und neben Esch-sur-Alzette der wichtigste Industriestandort des Landes. Bei dem Wettbewerb Dudelange ging es darum, eine nachhaltige urbane Verdichtung auf der Industriebrache zwischen den bestehenden Quartieren „Schmelz" und „Italien" zu gestalten und geschickt mit dem Bestand zu vernetzen.

Cba schlagen gemeinsam mit Latz und Partner sowie R+T verkehrsplaner dafür ein Straßennetz vor, das sich aus der orthogonalen Struktur der Untergrundbauwerke ableitet und mit neuen Ost-West-Verbindungen zwischen „Schmelz" und „Italien" verwoben wird. Dadurch werden die beiden

VIEW TO THE SAUER RIVER VALLEY AT THE B7 CROSSING

of the subterranean buildings, interwoven with the new east-west connections between "Schmelz" and "Italy." In this way, both urban quarters are to be linked with each other. The railway station Dudelange Usine is envisaged to obtain a new station square while a redesigned entrance will mark the approach to the new quarter. The planners are proposing to shift the Route de Thionville close to the railway line in order to reconnect the former slag heap with the city, creating a leafy promenade between the main traffic route and the city.

The number of floors in the buildings of this mixed zone steadily decreases as one goes from the Route de Thionville to the periphery. The mix of apartment buildings and detached as well as semidetached houses makes the area lively and cosmopolitan. The existing ensemble consisting of a water tower, administrative buildings, workshops, and halls forms something of an urban anchor for the site and its residents. A series of squares with shops, cafes, restaurants, and a school serves to enliven the area. Water basins mark the changeover to the "Schmelzpark."

Formerly, blast furnaces determined the sil-

et R+T verkehrsplaner, propose pour cela un réseau de voies calé sur les substructures existantes et leur orthogonalité, s'entrelaçant habilement avec la nouvelle liaison est-ouest entre « Schmelz » et « Italie ». La gare de Dudelange-Usines est requalifiée grâce à l'aménagement d'une nouvelle place bordée par un signal urbain fort, marquant l'entrée du nouveau quartier. L'équipe d'urbanistes propose de déplacer la route de Thionville et de l'accoler à la voie ferrée afin de pouvoir relier l'ancien crassier à la ville et former une promenade de verdure entre l'axe à grande circulation et cette dernière.

Le nombre de niveaux des bâtiments de la zone mixte mêlant résidentiel et activités va en diminuant depuis la route de Thionville vers l'extérieur de la zone. À cette mixité des fonctions s'ajoute une mixité sociale, par le mélange d'immeubles d'habitation et de maisons uni- ou bi-familiales. L'ensemble existant constitué du château d'eau, de bâtiments administratifs, d'ateliers et de hangars donne à ce lieu une identité propre. Une succession de places avec des magasins, des cafés, des restaurants et une école devrait créer de l'animation et apporter de

Viertel miteinander verbunden. Der Bahnhof Dudelange-Usines soll durch einen neuen Bahnhofsplatz aufgewertet werden und ein städtebaulicher Akzent den Eingang des neuen Quartiers markieren. Die Planer schlagen vor, die Route de Thionville an die Bahntrasse zu verlegen, um die ehemalige Schlackenhalde an die Stadt anzubinden und eine grüne Promenade zwischen Hauptverkehrsachse und Stadt bilden zu können.

Die Geschossanzahl des Mischgebiets verringert sich von der Route de Thionville nach außen. Die Mischung aus Geschosswohnungsbauten sowie Ein- bis Zweifamilienhäusern erlaubt außerdem eine soziale Durchmischung. Das bestehende Ensemble aus Wasserturm, Verwaltungsgebäuden, Werkstätten und Hallen stiftet dem Ort Identität. Eine Abfolge von Plätzen mit Läden, Cafés und Restaurants sowie einer Schule soll den Bereich beleben; Wasserbecken bilden den Übergang zum „Schmelzpark".

Traditionell bestimmten die Hochöfen die Stadtsilhouette von Dudelange. Die Planer wollen die axiale Verbindung dieses Standorts zum Walzwerk als visuellen Bezug zu „Klein-Italien" nutzen. Aus der Orientierung

MASTER PLAN DUDELANGE SCHMELZ | AERIAL VIEW OF THE SITE

houette of the city of Dudelange. The planners envisage using the axial connection between the site and the rolling mill as visual reference to "Little Italy," viewing the integrative character of the urban axis as a vital tool for creating a sense of orientation in the urban mix. As such, the ground plans of the blast furnaces become constitutive aesthetic criteria of the streetscapes. For the area adjacent to the "Schmelzpark," the planners have earmarked a mixed zone comprising residential and service uses as well as daily supply facilities. The hollowed out rolling mill whose columns and large parts of the roof are being preserved, will be turned into a flexible structure for new commercial uses. The development plan of the open and green spaces follows three types: the Route de Thionville forms the spine for the urban streets, paths, and squares with their alleys and structured tree clusters. The historical industrial green belt is determined by the course of the railway line and is characterized by freely arranged groups of trees. Lined by willow and alder trees, the promenade snugly fits to the stream of the new Düdelingen creek. The Cours des Hauts-

la vie. La transition avec le « Schmelzpark » est assurée par un ensemble de bassins.
La silhouette traditionnelle de Dudelange était celle de ses hauts fourneaux. Aussi cba se propose-t-il d'utiliser comme ligne de force – renvoyant, plus loin, à la « Petite Italie » – l'axe reliant leur ancien emplacement au laminoir. Tel qu'il se situe dans le tissu urbain, cet axe devient un espace-clé de la viabilisation. La trace des hauts fourneaux peut alors être reprise comme attribut caractéristique de la voirie. Donnant sur le Schmelzpark, l'équipe prévoit également un ensemble mixte mêlant logements, commerces de proximité et services. Le bâtiment du laminoir, vidé et dont subsistent les poteaux et une grande partie de la toiture, devient un ouvrage transparent, flexible, pour des usages commerciaux et tertiaires. Pour les espaces extérieurs, cba distingue trois types de traitement paysager. La route de Thionville forme l'épine dorsale du réseau viaire, des chemins et des places : les arbres y sont strictement alignés en allées ou ordonnés en bosquets. La « coulée verte » liée à l'histoire industrielle du lieu se développe sur la trace des embranchements

im Stadtgefüge greifen sie die Achse als Erschließungsraum auf. Die Grundrisse der Hochöfen können so zum Gestaltungsmerkmal des Straßenraums werden. Im Anschluss an den Schmelzpark sehen die Planer eine Mischnutzung aus Wohnen, Nahversorgungseinrichtungen und Dienstleistungen vor. Aus dem entkernten Walzwerk, dessen Stützen und große Teile des Daches erhalten bleiben, wird eine durchlässige, flexibel nutzbare Struktur für gewerbliche Nutzungen.
Für die Entwicklung der Freiräume unterscheiden die Planer drei Typen: Die Route de Thionville bildet das Rückgrat für die urbanen Straßen, Wege und Plätze mit Alleen und geordneten Baumhainen. Der industriehistorische Grünzug entwickelt sich aus den Gleistrassen und wird durch frei angeordnete Baumgruppen charakterisiert. Von Weiden und Erlen gesäumt, präsentiert sich die Promenade am neuen Düdelinger Bach. Der „Cours des Hauts-Fourneaux" ist geprägt durch eine mittige Promenade, die von Wasser und Bäumen umgeben ist.
Wasser wird vor allem in den Klär- und Kühlbecken sichtbar, die den Freiraum bestim-

VIEW FROM "LITTLE ITALY" TO THE "SCHMELZPARK"

Fourneaux is shaped by a central promenade surrounded by water and trees.

The sedimentation tanks and cooling ponds in particular make the element of water visible to the outside. They determine the look of the open spaces and act as a kind of "water park." The traffic plan has the aim of avoiding car journeys, while providing the residents and employees of the area with attractive alternatives to the car. Parking spaces have been reduced to a minimum.

The new urban quarter is to become a model of sustainable city planning with its high density, its sophisticated design of open spaces, the preservation of historical buildings, the green roofs, its block heating station, solar plant, and eco-center.

ferroviaires : elle se caractérise par des arbres groupés librement. La promenade le long du nouveau cours du ruisseau de Dudelange, traitée dans le même esprit, est bordée de saules et d'aulnes. Enfin, le « Cours des Hauts-Fourneaux » comporte dans son axe une promenade avec des arbres et des bassins.

L'eau est surtout présente avec les bassins de décantation et de trempe, éléments-clés des espaces extérieurs et qui font office de jardin d'eau. Le schéma de circulation de la zone vise à éviter l'usage des voitures et à offrir aux habitants et aux personnes travaillant dans le quartier des alternatives attrayantes à l'automobile. De ce fait, les places de stationnement sont limitées à un minimum.

Une densité urbaine élevée, des espaces extérieurs de qualité, la conservation des constructions existantes, des toitures végétalisées, des installations de chauffage solaire et un centre de tri doivent faire de ce nouveau quartier un exemple d'urbanisme durable.

men und als „Wasserpark" fungieren. Ziel des Verkehrskonzeptes ist es, Autofahrten zu vermeiden und den Bewohnern und Beschäftigten des Gebiets attraktive Alternativen zum Auto zu bieten. Der Parkraum wird auf ein Minimum beschränkt.

Die hohe Dichte, qualitätvolle Außenräume, der Erhalt von Bausubstanz, Gründächer, ein Blockheizkraftwerk, Solaranlage und ein Eco-Center sollen den neuen Stadtteil zu einem Beispiel für nachhaltigen Städtebau machen.

PARTNER

Louis Edmond NICOLAS

1948 born in Philippeville, Belgium. Studied architecture from the Institut d'Architecture Saint-Luc in Tournai, Belgium. 1972 degree. 1972 internship in the architecture firm Yves Lepère in Wahlain-St.Paul. 1975 architect for project on the state school building stock in Arlon, Belgium. 1988 architect in the office of Christian Bauer. Since 1997 partner in the firm christian bauer & associés architectes s.c.

Né en 1948 à Philippeville (B) ; études d'architecture à l'Institut d'Architecture Saint-Luc à Tournai (B), diplômé en 1972. 1972 stage d'architecture auprès du cabinet d'architecture Yves Lepère à Wahlain-St.Paul; 1975 architecte au Fonds des Bâtiments Scolaires de l'État à Arlon (B) ; 1988 architecte au cabinet d'architecture Christian Bauer Architecte. Depuis 1997 : architecte associé au cabinet d'architecture christian bauer & associés architectes s.c.

1948 geboren in Philippeville (B); Architekturstudium am Institut d'Architecture Saint-Luc in Tournai (B), 1972 Abschlussdiplom. 1972 Praktikum im Architekturbüro Yves Lepère in Wahlain-St.Paul; 1975 Architekt für staatlichen Schulgebäudebestand in Arlon (B); 1988 Architekt im Büro Christian Bauer. Seit 1997 Partnerarchitekt im Büro christian bauer & associés architectes s.c.

Norbert MULLER

1956 born in Luxembourg. Studied civil engineering and architecture at the University of Liège, Belgium. 1981 degree. 1981 architect with "Groupe Tetra," Luxembourg-Helfent; 1982 architect for his own projects; 1983 architect in the office of Pierre Bohler, Luxembourg; 1987 architect in the office of Christian Bauer in Bridel, Luxembourg. Since 1990 partner in the firm christian bauer & associés architectes.

Né en 1956 à Luxembourg ; études d'ingénieur civil architecte à l'université de Liège (B), diplômé en 1981 1981 architecte au sein du Groupe Tetra, Luxembourg-Helfent ; 1982 projets individuels ; 1983 architecte au sein du cabinet de M. Pierre Bohler, Luxembourg-Ville ; 1987 architecte au sein du cabinet de M. Christian Bauer, Bridel (L). Depuis 1990

architecte associé au cabinet d'architecture christian bauer & associés architectes.

1956 geboren in Luxemburg (L); Bauingenieur-Architekturstudium an der Universität von Lüttich (B), 1981 Abschlussdiplom; 1981 Architekt bei „Groupe Tetra", Luxemburg-Helfent (L); 1982 eigene Projekte; 1983 Architekt im Büro Pierre Bohler, Luxemburg (L); 1987 Architekt im Büro Christian Bauer, Bridel (L). Seit 1990 Partnerarchitekt im Büro christian bauer & associés architectes

Michael FEISTHAUER

1968 born in Trier, Germany. Studied architecture at the University of Applied Sciences in Trier. 1994 degree. 1994 architect in the office of Heinrich Böll in Essen, Germany; 1997 collaboration with Martin A. Becker and Horst Schlösser in Cologne, Germany; 1997 architect in the office of christian bauer & associés architectes s.c. Since 2003 partner in the firm christian bauer & associés architectes s.a.

Né en 1968 à Trèves (D) ; études d'architecture à la Fachhochschule de Trèves, diplômé en 1994. 1994 architecte au sein du cabinet Heinrich Böll, Essen (D) ; 1997 collaboration avec Martin A. Becker et Horst Schlösser à Cologne (D) ; 1997 architecte dans le cabinet d'architecture christian bauer & associés architectes s.c. Depuis 2003 : architecte associé au cabinet d'architecture christian bauer & associés architectes s.a.

1968 geboren in Trier (D); Architekturstudium an der Fachhochschule in Trier, 1994 Abschlussdiplom. 1994 Architekt im Büro Heinrich Böll, Essen (D); 1997 Zusammenarbeit mit Martin A. Becker und Horst Schlösser in Köln (D); 1997 Architekt im Büro christian bauer & associés architectes s.c. Seit 2003 Partnerarchitekt im Büro christian bauer & associés architectes s.a.

Sala MAKUMBUNDU

1972 born in Bonn, Germany. Studied architecture at the University of Kaiserslautern, Germany, and at the École d'architecture in Nantes, France. 1998 degree from the University of Kaiserslautern. 1998 architect in the office of christian bauer & associés ar-

chitectes s.c. Since 2003 partner in the firm christian bauer & associés architectes s.a. Since September 2009 board member of the Chamber of Architects and Engineers.

Née en 1972 à Bonn (D) ; études d'architecture à l'Université de Kaiserslautern (D) et à l'Ecole d'architecture de Nantes (F), diplômée en 1998 à l'Université de Kaiserslautern. 1998 architecte au cabinet christian bauer & associés architectes s.c. Depuis 2003 : architecte associée du cabinet christian bauer & associés architectes s.a. Membre du Conseil de l'Ordre des Architectes et des Ingénieurs-Conseils depuis septembre 2009.

1972 geboren in Bonn (D); Architekturstudium an der Universität in Kaiserslautern (D) und an der Ecole d'architecture von Nantes (F), 1998 Abschlussdiplom an der Universität von Kaiserslautern. 1998 Architektin innerhalb des Büros christian bauer & associés architectes s.c. Seit 2003 Partnerarchitektin im Büro christian bauer & associés architectes s.a. Seit September 2009 Vorstandsmitglied in der Kammer für Architekten und Ingenieure.

COLLABORATORS 1988–2010
COLLABORATEURS 1988–2010
MITARBEITER 1988–2010

Pit Freilinger, Sabine Kleker, Guy Mouriamé, Daniel Reinert, Nicolas Stöber, Thomas Kruppa, Guido Mertesdorf, Inga Bischoff, Corentin Emprou, Claudine Jungbluth, Johannes Bäuerlein, Achim Bursch, Frank Murawski, Nadine Nettbohl, Lisa Neisius, Roland Hermann, Wolfgang Taphorn, Sofie Borré, Delphine Haluk, Ode Vigneron, Anne Goicoétchéa, Philippe Dehebert, Marion Diederich, Fabrizio Raspanti, Frank Stolz, Marianne Hilpert, Anne Bastgen, Jo Nei, Ulrich Bachmann, Joachim Weber, Andreas Klöpfer, Erwin Leus, Joël Cavallaro, Maud Jacob, Kai Hofmann, Frank Nicklas, Eric Vallenet, Michel Heisbourg, Carlos Correia, Carole Pax, Senad Vrazlacic, Denis Ertaz, Daniel Brückmann, André Nabulon, Heike Meyer Rotsch, Harald Groll, Jeannette Sinnes, Sophie Gredt, Jean Paul De Waha, Anne Deverth, Tom Beiler, Felipe de Pimentel, Heike Schmitt, Rainer Roth, James Cumming, Romain Bouschet, Christiane Kuborn, Fabienne Dalo

Christian BAUER

1947 born in Luxembourg. 1974 degree in Architecture from ETH in Zurich, Switzerland. 1975 founded the Christian Bauer office; 1990 established christian bauer & associés architectes s.c. with partners Marie-Hélène Lucas and Norbert Muller; 1997–2002 ran christian bauer & associés architectes s.c with the partners Norbert Muller and Louis Edmond Nicolas. Since 2003 practice known as christian bauer & associés architectes s.a.
Since 2007 president of the Fondation de l'Architecture et l'Ingénieurie. 2008 curator of the Luxembourg architecture biennale in Venice. Member and president of various architecture competition juries.

Né en 1947 à Luxembourg. Études d'architecture à l'école polytechnique fédérale à Zurich (CH), diplômé en 1974. 1975 création du bureau Christian Bauer ; 1990 création du bureau christian bauer & associés architectes s.c. avec les associés Marie-Hélène Lucas et Norbert Muller ; de 1997 à 2002 christian bauer & associés architectes s.c. avec les associés Norbert Muller et Louis Edmond Nicolas. Depuis 2003 : bureau dans la configuration actuelle sous le nom de christian bauer & associés architectes s.a.
Depuis 2007, président de la Fondation de l'Architecture et de l'Ingénierie. Curateur pour le Luxembourg pour la Biennale de l'architecture Venise 2008. Membre et président de différents jurys de concours d'architecture.

1947 geboren in Luxemburg (L). Architekturstudium an der ETH in Zürich (CH), 1974 Abschlussdiplom. 1975 Gründung des Büros Christian Bauer; 1990 Gründung des Büros christian bauer & associés architectes s.c. mit den Partnern Marie-Hélène Lucas und Norbert Muller; 1997 bis 2002 christian bauer & associés architectes s.c mit den Partnern Norbert Muller und Louis Edmond Nicolas. Seit 2003 Büro in aktueller Konstellation unter der Bezeichnung christian bauer & associés architectes s.a.
Seit 2007 Präsident der Fondation de l'Architecture et l'Ingénieurie. Kurator der Architekturbiennale Venedig 2008 für Luxemburg. Mitglied und Präsident in verschiedenen Jurys von Architekturwettbewerben.

TWELVE QUESTIONS

Ulf Meyer (UM) Mr. Bauer, you are a globetrotter and a global citizen. Would you describe yourself as a Luxembourger architect or as an architect who happens to be working in Luxembourg?

Christian Bauer (CB) I am a Luxembourger architect. But, as an architect, I want to represent the new Luxembourg. This is because the country is rapidly changing. It has become more international and has a strong European identity. This has to do with the banks, the EU institutions and the geographical position of Luxembourg. Like many Luxembourg citizens, I like to travel and to see the country from outside, so that I can ask myself: who are we Luxembourgers? When I returned from my study period at the ETH in Zurich, many colleagues asked me why I wanted to return to "tiny Luxembourg." I wanted to return as I saw many opportunities in my homeland. There were no strict building regulations and an abundance of clients. My first clients had been Europeans. They took an interest in architecture. The ordinary Luxem-

Ulf Meyer (UM) Monsieur Bauer, vous êtes un voyageur du monde, un citoyen du monde. Mais êtes-vous un architecte luxembourgeois ? Ou bien êtes-vous simplement un architecte que le hasard a conduit à travailler au Luxembourg ?

Christian Bauer (CB) Je suis un architecte luxembourgeois. Mais, à ce titre, je souhaiterais représenter le « Luxembourg nouveau ». Car le pays se transforme ; il a acquis une nouvelle identité européenne et une dimension internationale forte. Ceci est lié à la fois à la présence des banques et des institutions européennes et à la situation géographique du pays. Comme beaucoup de Luxembourgeois, j'aime voyager, pour avoir une vision de l'extérieur sur ce pays et pouvoir m'interroger sur qui nous sommes, nous les Luxembourgeois.

Quand je suis revenu ici après mes études à l'EPF de Zurich, beaucoup de collègues m'ont demandé pourquoi je voulais retourner au Luxembourg, un « petit » pays. Les perspectives me paraissaient intéressantes, sans règlements de construction restrictifs et avec une clientèle nombreuse. Mes premiers maîtres d'ouvrage furent « européens ». Ils s'intéressaient à

Ulf Meyer (UM) Herr Bauer, Sie sind ein Weltreisender und Weltbürger, sind Sie auch ein *Luxemburger* Architekt? Oder sind Sie ein Architekt, der zufällig in Luxemburg arbeitet?

Christian Bauer (CB) Ich bin ein Luxemburger Architekt. Aber ich möchte ein Architekt sein, der das neue Luxemburg vertritt. Denn das Land verändert sich, ist internationaler geworden und hat eine starke europäische Identität. Das hat mit den Banken, den EU-Institutionen und der geografischen Lage Luxemburgs zu tun. Wie viele Luxemburger reise ich gerne, um den Blick von außen auf Luxemburg zu haben und um mich zu fragen: Wer sind wir Luxemburger? Als ich nach meiner Studienzeit an der ETH aus Zürich zurückkam, fragten mich viele Kollegen, warum ich denn in das „kleine Luxemburg" zurückgehen wollte. Ich sah eine gute Chance in meinem Heimatland, denn es gab keine strengen Bauvorschriften und viele Kunden. Meine

bourger was not in the habit of commissioning architects at the time. My clients respected architecture. During those early years, there existed a sophisticated architectural culture in the countries around Luxembourg but not in the country itself. This has gradually changed for the better.

UM Was there also a sense of loss that Luxembourg has felt during this process?

CB It has gained more than it has lost. Indeed, it has lost something: I am upset about the bad architecture in the villages. But perhaps more important is the issue of scale: we can now find many more shapeless "blocks" devoid of any sense of scale than was the case before. We once had homogeneous villages in Luxembourg, but they have mostly been spoilt.

UM The one foreign country you took inspiration from was Switzerland, wasn't it?

CB Yes, of course! My early designs were much inspired by Le Corbusier. Le Corbusier had had an ideology and I can very well understand that: when one wants to plan a revolution, one cannot do things by halves. One has to be radical. But it was also Lucius Burckhardt at the ETH who influenced me. With the appearance of postmodernism, important questions were also being asked in Switzerland. Even Le Corbusier was called into question in the nineteen-sixties. At the time, I was interested in postmodern thinkers and designers such as Robert Venturi, Ricardo Bofill, Charles Moore, and James Stirling. Modernism, the International Style, had been corrupted by bad imitations. The same drab "boxes" were built all over the world.

I then made the acquaintance of Rob and Leon Krier. Their postmodern approaches, their questioning of modernism, fascinated me. As a result, my own work became more urban. This was also because postmodernism viewed architecture as being the principal building block of the city. But this was precisely the weakness of modernism: it has produced fascinating shapes and sculptures but no good urban planning, no appropriate streets and squares. Postmodernism began with urban planning. Respect for history was also a postmodern achievement. Postmodern ground plans were no longer exclusively determined by functional considerations but also by their figurative meanings and suitability for creating more comfortable

l'architecture. Le Luxembourgeois moyen d'alors n'allait pas voir un architecte. Mes clients, eux, étaient respectueux de l'architecture. À l'époque, une culture de l'architecture existait tout autour du Luxembourg, mais pas encore chez nous. Depuis cette époque, l'environnement au Luxembourg n'a cessé de s'améliorer.

UM Ce faisant, le Luxembourg a-t-il aussi perdu quelque chose ?

CB Il a gagné plus qu'il n'a perdu. Mais il a aussi perdu : la mauvaise architecture dans les villages m'irrite terriblement, mais plus encore le manque de proportion, d'échelle, pourtant essentielles. On construit beaucoup de « boîtes à chaussures ». Le Luxembourg avait autrefois des villages homogènes, mais beaucoup se sont désormais terriblement enlaidis.

UM La Suisse a constitué votre première influence étrangère …

CB Bien sûr ! Mes premiers projets étaient encore influencés par Le Corbusier. Le Corbusier avait une idéologie, ce que je conçois parfaitement car, si on prépare la révolution, on ne peut pas faire les choses à moitié, on doit être radical. Mais j'ai aussi été marqué par Lucius Burkhardt, qui intervenait à l'EPF. Avec l'apparition du postmodernisme, beaucoup de questions importantes étaient soulevées en Suisse, et même Le Corbusier y était remis en question dans les années 1960. À l'époque aussi, je me suis intéressé à Robert Venturi et à d'autres penseurs et architectes postmodernes comme Ricardo Bofill, Charles Moore et James Stirling. Le modernisme, le style international, étaient alors corrompus par de mauvaises copies. Partout dans le monde, on retrouvait les mêmes boîtes.

J'ai alors fait la connaissance de Rob et Leon Krier. Leurs approches postmodernes, la remise en question du modernisme, m'ont captivé. Mon travail a pris de ce fait une forme plus urbanistique. Le postmodernisme voyait en effet l'architecture comme une composante de la ville – tandis que l'urbanisme avait été le point faible du modernisme. Le modernisme a produit des formes et des sculptures fascinantes, mais pas de bon urbanisme, pas de rues ni de places agréables. Le postmodernisme a commencé par l'urbanisme. Le respect pour l'histoire est aussi une acquisition du postmodernisme. Les plans postmodernes n'étaient plus déterminés uniquement par la fonction, mais aussi par la forme et ils étaient faciles à vivre. Aujourd'hui,

ersten Bauherren waren Europäer. *Die* haben sich für Architektur interessiert. Der normale Luxemburger ist damals nicht zum Architekten gegangen. Meine Kunden hatten Respekt vor Architektur. Damals gab es Architektur-Kultur rund um Luxemburg herum, aber noch nicht im Land selbst. Das Umfeld in Luxemburg hat sich seitdem immer besser entwickelt.

UM Hat Luxemburg dabei auch etwas verloren?

CB Es hat mehr gewonnen als verloren. Aber es verliert auch: Ich rege mich auf über die schlechte Architektur in den Dörfern, aber noch wichtiger ist die Maßstäblichkeit: Jetzt werden viele maßstabslose „Klötze" gebaut. Wir hatten einmal homogene Dörfer in Luxemburg, aber viele sind jetzt lädiert.

UM Ihr Auslandseinfluss war in erster Linie die Schweiz …

CB Ja, natürlich! Meine ersten Entwürfe waren noch von Le Corbusier beeinflusst. Le Corbusier hatte eine Ideologie und das kann ich gut nachvollziehen: Wenn man eine Revolution plant, kann man keine halben Dinge machen, dann muss man radikal sein. Aber auch Lucius Burckhardts Wirken an der ETH hat mich damals geprägt. Man hat auch in der Schweiz mit dem Aufkommen der Postmoderne wichtige Fragen gestellt, selbst Le Corbusier wurde in den sechziger Jahren infrage gestellt. Ich habe mich damals für Robert Venturi und andere postmoderne Denker und Entwerfer wie Ricardo Bofill, Charles Moore und James Stirling interessiert. Die Moderne, der International Style, war in den sechziger Jahren durch das schlechte Kopieren korrumpiert. Es gab überall auf der Welt dieselben Kästen.

Ich habe dann Rob und Leon Krier kennengelernt. Ihre postmodernen Ansätze, das Infragestellen der Moderne, haben mich fasziniert. Meine Arbeit wurde dadurch städtebaulicher, denn die Postmoderne sah Architektur als Baustein der Stadt. Genau da lag aber die Schwäche der Moderne: Sie hat faszinierende Figuren und Skulpturen hervorgebracht, aber keinen guten Städtebau, keine angenehmen Straßen und Plätze. Die Postmoderne hat mit dem Städtebau angefangen, auch der Respekt vor der Geschichte war eine Errungenschaft der Postmoderne. Die postmodernen Grundrisse waren nicht mehr nur von der Funktionalität geprägt, sondern von der Figur und gut zum Wohnen geeignet. Heute, fast 40 Jahre nach meinem Studium, interessiere ich mich abermals für die Schweizer Baukunst, wo der Minimalismus blüht. Künstler der Minimal Art wie Dan Flavin, Carl André oder Donald Judd begeistern und inspirieren mich. Nur wenigen Entwerfern gelingt es jedoch, Minimalismus so geschickt in Raumkunst umzusetzen wie Erwin Heerich beispielsweise. Auch in Japan findet die Tradition der Reduktion heute in dem Werk von Architekten wie Kengo Kuma oder Kazuyo Sejima einen ungemein attraktiven, neuen Ausdruck, von dem ich mich gerne beeinflussen lasse.

UM Wann – und vor allem warum – haben Sie mit der Postmoderne gebrochen? War das Museum in Luxemburg für Sie das erste Gebäude einer neuen Generation?

lives. Today, almost forty years after my studies, Swiss architecture has again begun to interest me, particularly for its minimalism. Artists of Minimal Art such as Dan Flavin, Carl André, or Donald Judd captivate and inspire me. However, there are only a few artists who succeed in translating Minimalism into space as adeptly as Erwin Heerich, for example. I've also been inspired by the Japanese tradition of minimalism that finds expression in the work of architects such as Kengo Kuma and Kazuyo Sejima.

UM When and why did you break away from postmodernism? Was the museum in Luxembourg the first building of a new generation?

CB No, it was the first residential building that I had built for myself. There was no external client for that project.

UM Your work is unusual and agreeably diverse in terms of building typologies. You have designed villas and museums, but also large office buildings. You are also engaged with urban planning. Only a select few architects have the talent and organizational skills to be involved with so many different typologies. Do you reject specialization? Have you consciously diversified to include so many different typologies?

CB One has to be able to do everything! A good architect does not necessarily need a lot of experience. Just think of the Centre Pompidou in Paris: it turned out so convincingly because the architects were so young and inexperienced. A new view of things helps. Quite often, a fresh approach wins over experience.

UM Is there a type of building you have always wanted to design?

CB I would really like to design an interconnected, homogeneous urban quarter. Not just objects, but interrelations! In the early days, I was not much interested in urban planning. I only discovered this field through my practice as urban planning consultant for the Kirchberg. In recent times, however, we have been rather successful with urban planning projects, such as the one in Dudelange or in the "Nordstad," where we sensitively engaged with the context of the place.

près de 40 ans après mes études, je continue à m'intéresser à l'architecture suisse, où le minimalisme fait florès. Les artistes minimalistes comme Dan Flavin, Carl André ou Donald Judd, me ravissent également et m'inspirent. Peu de créateurs sont parvenus à traduire aussi habilement le minimalisme en volume que ne l'a fait Erwin Heerich, par exemple. Au Japon aussi, la tradition de la réduction trouve aujourd'hui une nouvelle expression extraordinairement attrayante, par laquelle je me laisse volontiers influencer, avec le travail d'architectes comme Kengo Kuma ou Kazuyo Sejima.

UM Quand, et surtout pourquoi, avez-vous rompu avec le postmodernisme ? Le Musée national d'histoire et d'art de Luxembourg a-t-il été pour vous le premier bâtiment d'une nouvelle génération ?

CB Non, c'est plutôt à l'occasion de la première maison d'habitation que j'ai construite, pour moi-même. Là, je n'avais pas de client.

UM Votre œuvre est inhabituellement et agréablement multiple et variée : vous avez construit des villas, des musées, de grands immeubles de bureaux ; vous faites aussi de l'urbanisme. Peu d'architectes maîtrisent autant de typologies différentes, que l'on se réfère à votre talent comme à votre organisation. Rejetez-vous toute spécialisation ? Est-ce un choix délibéré ?

CB On doit tout savoir faire ! Un bon architecte n'a pas nécessairement besoin de beaucoup d'expérience. Pensez au Centre Pompidou, à Paris : ça a été une telle réussite, parce que les architectes étaient alors jeunes et inexpérimentés. Un regard neuf aide. Souvent, la fraîcheur l'emporte sur l'expérience.

UM Y a-t-il un type de bâtiments que vous auriez toujours voulu construire ?

CB J'aimerais bien construire une fois un quartier urbain complet, dans sa continuité et son homogénéité. Pas seulement des bâtiments ici ou là, mais du lien ! Au début, je ne me suis pas particulièrement intéressé à l'urbanisme, je n'y suis venu qu'avec le regard que j'ai été amené à porter sur le Kirchberg. J'y suis venu avec conviction, et ces derniers temps nous avons eu pas mal de succès avec des projets d'urbanisme, comme à Dudelange ou dans la « Nordstad », où nous avons abordé le contexte de manière sensible.

CB Nein, das war das erste Wohnhaus, das ich für mich selbst gebaut habe. Da hatte ich keinen Kunden.

UM Ihr Werk ist ungewöhnlich und angenehm vielfältig, was die Bauaufgaben betrifft. Sie haben Villen, Museen, aber auch große Bürohäuser gebaut und beschäftigen sich mit Städtebau. Nur wenige Architekten beherrschen so viele verschiedene Typologien, was ihr Talent und ihre Organisation betrifft. Lehnen Sie Spezialisierung ab? Haben Sie das bewusst betrieben?

CB Man muss alles können! Ein guter Architekt braucht nicht unbedingt viel Erfahrung. Denken Sie an das Centre Pompidou in Paris: Es ist so gut gelungen, weil die Architekten damals so jung und unerfahren waren. Der neue Blick hilft. Oft schlägt die frische Herangehensweise die Erfahrung.

UM Gibt es einen Gebäudetypus, den sie schon immer mal bauen wollten?

CB Ich würde gerne einmal ein zusammenhängendes, homogenes Stadtviertel bauen. Nicht nur Objekte, sondern Zusammenhänge! Anfangs habe ich mich für den Städtebau nicht besonders interessiert und kam erst durch die Planungen für den Kirchberg dazu. In letzter Zeit sind wir aber mit städtebaulichen Entwürfen recht erfolgreich gewesen, zum Beispiel in Dudelange oder in der „Nordstad", wo wir sensibel auf den Kontext eingegangen sind.

UM Ist städtebauliches Entwerfen etwas grundsätzlich anderes oder kann man sagen „ein Raum ähnelt einem Haus, ein Haus ähnelt einem Quartier, ein Quartier ähnelt einer Stadt" und der Maßstab ist gar nicht so wichtig?

CB Bei Kollegen habe ich beobachtet, dass manche zwar gute Hochbauentwürfe machen, aber weniger guten Städtebau. Die architektonische Fokussierung auf das Objekt kommt von der Selbstdarstellung des Eigentums. Mich interessiert der Kontext viel mehr. Ein Gebäude ist nichts Privates, denn selbst ein Privathaus ist keine reine Privatangelegenheit, weil viele Menschen es sehen und es seine Umwelt prägt.

UM Herr Nicolas, gibt es Architekten, die Sie besonders beeinflusst haben?

Louis Edmond Nicolas (LN) Das Denken und die Architektur von Louis I. Kahn waren für mich als Student eine Entdeckung, die bis heute meine Überlegungen beeinflusst. Die Geometrie und die Unterscheidung zwischen dienenden und bedienten Räumen haben damals mein Interesse geweckt. Dieser Einfluss hat sich noch verstärkt, als ich meine berufliche Laufbahn bei Yves Lepère begann. Die Arbeit im Grundriss, die Materialität, das Licht, die poetische und symbolische Dimension einer kontextuellen und zeitlosen Architektur gehören auch zu meinen Ansätzen. Eine Reise nach Japan Ende der neunziger Jahre, bei der ich unter anderem Projekte von Tadao Ando und Fumihiko Maki sowie die kaiserliche Villa Katsura besuchte, hat die Suche nach der Reduzierung auf das Wesentliche noch verstärkt.

UM Wodurch wurden Sie als Architekt beeinflusst, Herr Feisthauer?

UM Is urban planning fundamentally different from architecture or does, indeed, the following statement hold true: "a room resembles a house; a house resembles an urban quarter; and an urban quarter resembles a city"? Is the issue of scale of secondary importance?

CB I have observed that some colleagues of mine are able to design good buildings but don't succeed in creating good urban planning. The architectural obsession with the object comes from a sort of self-portrayal of ownership. I am, however, more interested in the issue of context. A building does not strictly represent something entirely private because even a private residence finds itself in a public realm: many people can see it and it does shape its wider environment in many ways.

UM Mr. Nicolas, are there architects who have particularly influenced you?

Louis Edmond Nicolas (LN) The thoughts and architecture of Louis Kahn were a great discovery for me as a young student and continue to shape me to this day. Geometry and the differentiation between serviced and service spaces had aroused my interest early on. This influence became even stronger after I started my professional career with Yves Lepère. Working with ground plans, materiality, light, and the poetic and symbolic dimensions of contextual and timeless architecture are also part of my approach. During a trip to Japan at the end of the nineteen-nineties, I visited buildings designed by Tadao Ando and Fumihiko Maki as well as the imperial villa Katsura. This strengthened my belief in distilling the essence of architecture through minimalism.

UM Mr. Feisthauer, who or what has shaped you as an architect?

Michael Feisthauer (MF) Professionally, my time in Essen was a great influence, where I had worked with the architects Heinrich Böll and Hans Krabel. Their contextual examination of brownfield sites and their buildings in the Ruhr region that were constructed following World War Two also became the focus of my work. I was also involved with the project to reanimate the historic Zeche Zollverein in Essen and convert a listed office building dating from the

UM L'urbanisme constitue-il un exercice totalement différent ou peut-on parler d'analogie entre la pièce et la maison, entre la maison et le quartier, entre le quartier et la ville ? L'échelle n'est-elle pas si importante que cela ?

CB J'ai observé chez certains collègues qu'ils produisaient de bons projets de bâtiments, mais de moins bonnes formes urbaines. Cette focalisation de l'architecture sur le bâtiment considéré en soi vient de la fonction de représentation qu'on accorde à la propriété privée. Ce qui m'intéresse bien plus, moi, c'est l'environnement. Un bâtiment n'est en rien privé. Même une maison privée n'est pas une affaire purement privée, parce que beaucoup de gens la voient et qu'elle marque son environnement.

UM Monsieur Nicolas, y a-t-il des architectes qui vous ont particulièrement influencé ?

Louis Edmond Nicolas (LN) Lorsque j'étais encore étudiant, la pensée et l'architecture de Louis Kahn ont été pour moi une révélation qui influence aujourd'hui encore mes réflexions. À l'époque, la géométrie et la distinction entre espaces servis et espaces servants m'ont intéressé. Cette influence s'est encore renforcée lorsque j'ai commencé ma carrière professionnelle chez Yves Lepère. Le travail sur le plan, la matérialité, la lumière, la dimension poétique et symbolique d'une architecture contextuelle et intemporelle appartiennent aussi à mes approches. Un voyage au Japon à la fin des années 1990, au cours duquel j'ai visité, entre autres, la villa impériale Katsura ainsi que des projets de Tadao Ando et de Fumihiko Maki, a encore renforcé ma recherche de la réduction à l'essentiel.

UM Monsieur Feisthauer, par quelles influences l'architecte que vous êtes a-t-il été modelé ?

Michael Feisthauer (MF) Mon passage à Essen et ma collaboration avec les architectes Heinrich Böll et Hans Krabel m'ont profondément marqué professionnellement. J'ai participé à leurs côtés à la revitalisation de la friche minière du Zollverein à Essen et à la transformation d'un immeuble de bureaux des années 1950 classé monument historique. Ce fut l'occasion de partager leur approche contextuelle des friches industrielles et des témoins de l'architecture d'après-guerre du bassin de la Ruhr.

La manière claire, honnête et directe de travailler et d'agir de Heinrich Böll m'a donné, outre un vocabulaire architectonique de base, le bagage qui m'accompagne encore aujourd'hui.

Michael Feisthauer (MF) Meine berufliche Prägung erfuhr ich in Essen durch die Zusammenarbeit mit den Architekten Heinrich Böll und Hans Krabel. Deren kontextuelle Auseinandersetzung mit Industriebrachen und architektonischen Zeugnissen der Nachkriegsarchitektur im Ruhrgebiet war ebenfalls Thema meiner Mitarbeit an der Wiederbelebung der Zeche Zollverein in Essen und dem Umbau eines denkmalgeschützten Bürogebäudes der fünfziger Jahre. Heinrich Bölls klare, ehrliche und direkte Art zu arbeiten und zu handeln gaben mir neben einem architektonischen Grundvokabular auch das Rüstzeug für meinen Weg bis heute.

Die dort erlernte Herangehensweise an konzeptionelle Themen, „alles so einfach wie möglich zu machen, aber nicht einfacher" ist eine ganz ähnliche Grundhaltung, wie die, die wir in unserem Büro heute pflegen.

UM Was ist wichtig für die Umsetzung des Entwurfs in die Wirklichkeit, Herr Muller?

Norbert Muller (NM) Mit meiner technisch ausgerichteten Ausbildung als Ingenieur-Architekt ist mein Aufgabengebiet vor allem die Umsetzung der Entwürfe in die Realität, die Werkplanung, Ausschreibung und Bauüberwachung. Bei diesen Arbeitsschritten gilt es, den Entwurfsgedanken mit viel Sorgfalt und Liebe zum Detail bis zur Vollendung weiterzuführen. Besonders wichtig ist die harmonische Beziehung zwischen Architekt, Bauherr und Unternehmen.

UM Das Büro cba arbeitet auch in den Nachbarländern. Ist die Erfahrung, in Luxemburg zu arbeiten, dabei hilfreich, Frau Makumbundu?

Sala Makumbundu (SM) Luxemburg ist für mich ein idealer Ort zum Leben und Arbeiten. Die Einflüsse, die mich während meines Architekturstudiums in Deutschland und Frankreich geprägt haben, kann ich hier verbinden. Aufgewachsen mit zwei grundverschiedenen Kulturen, bietet das kosmopolitische Umfeld Luxemburgs für mich einen inspirierenden Rahmen für meine Arbeit. Für unser Büro erleichtert die Kenntnis der verschiedenen Kulturen das Arbeiten über Luxemburgs Grenzen hinaus.

UM Herr Feisthauer, was denken Sie, wie das Büro cba in einigen Jahren strukturiert sein wird?

MF Der Generationswechsel ist von Christian Bauer schon sorgsam vorbereitet worden. Cba ist heute mit fünf Teilhabern ein Unternehmen, das sich unter einer gemeinsamen Idee zusammenfindet. Es funktioniert wie die Statik eines Gebäudes: Die „alten Partner" sind das Fundament, die „jungen" bauen darauf auf. Uns halten eine Vertrauensbasis, das Zusammenspiel der Kräfte sowie ein Wertekanon zusammen. Diese Werte zeugen von Unternehmenskultur und Identität, die für unsere Kunden wie für unsere Mitarbeiter spürbar sind. Ich glaube, dass uns diese Grundhaltung authentisch macht.

UM Vielen Dank für das Gespräch!

nineteen-fifties. Heinrich Böll's candid and direct manner of working and his architectural vocabulary prepared me for my own professional endeavors, accompanying me to this day.
It was there that I learned to approach conceptual issues keeping in mind the basic principle
of "making things as simple as possible, but not simpler," is similar to the guiding principle of
our own office.

UM What does one have to keep in mind when a design is to be actually built, Mr. Muller?

Norbert Muller (NM) As an architect-engineer from a technical background, it is my task to
translate designs into reality, a process that includes construction drawings, tendering, and
building supervision. During this phase, it is important to see the design idea through to its
realization with a great deal of care and love for detail. What is especially important is a harmonious relationship between the architect, the client and the customer company.

UM The cba practice also works in neighboring countries. Does the experience of practicing
in Luxembourg help when doing so, Ms Makumbundu?

Sala Makumbundu (SM) For me, Luxembourg is an ideal place to live and work. I can apply
the impressions and influences from my architectural education in Germany and France here.
Having grown up with two entirely different cultures, the cosmopolitan environment of Luxembourg offers an inspiring frame for my work. The knowledge of different cultures is an asset
for our office when we work abroad.

UM Mr. Feisthauer, how do you think the cba office will be structured in a few years time?

MF The change of generation has already been meticulously prepared by Christian Bauer.
cba today is a company with five partners who all share a common idea. It's like calculating
structures: the "old partners" make up the foundation while the "young" ones build on it. A
common basis for trust, the interplay of diverse forces and a shared canon of values bind us
together. These values are proof of a corporate culture and identity, something that is felt by
both our clients and our staff. I believe it is this basic attitude that makes us authentic.

UM Many thanks for this conversation.

Sa manière d'aborder le domaine de la conception architecturale – faire au plus simple, sans
simplisme – rejoint tout à fait celle que nous cultivons aujourd'hui dans notre cabinet.

UM Monsieur Muller, qu'est-ce qui est important pour qu'un projet prenne corps ?

Norbert Muller (NM) En tant qu'architecte-ingénieur, j'ai une formation technique. Par
conséquent, j'interviens principalement dans la concrétisation des projets, la réalisation des
dossiers d'exécution, la préparation des appels d'offres et la direction des travaux. Tout au long
de ces phases, il s'agit de donner forme à l'idée du projet, de la mener jusqu'à la réalisation
finale, son accomplissement, et ce, avec beaucoup d'attention et d'amour du détail. Il importe
surtout que les relations soient harmonieuses entre l'architecte, le maître d'ouvrage et les
entreprises.

UM Madame Makumbundu, le cabinet cba travaille aussi dans les pays voisins. Votre expérience luxembourgeoise vous sert-elle ?

Sala Makumbundu (SM) Le Luxembourg est pour moi un endroit idéal pour vivre et travailler.
Ici, je peux faire la jonction entre les influences qui m'ont marquées pendant mes études
d'architecture en Allemagne et en France. J'ai été élevée avec deux cultures fondamentale-
ment différentes, et l'environnement cosmopolite du Luxembourg m'offre un cadre stimu-
lant pour mon travail. Pour le cabinet, la connaissance des différentes cultures facilite le travail
en dehors des frontières luxembourgeoises.

UM Monsieur Feisthauer, comment voyez-vous l'organisation de cba dans quelques années ?

MF Le changement de génération a déjà été soigneusement préparé par Christian Bauer.
Avec ses cinq associés, cba est aujourd'hui une société qui se reconnaît dans une idée
commune. Cela fonctionne comme la statique d'un bâtiment : les « anciens » constituent
les fondations, sur lesquelles les « jeunes » s'appuient. Notre cohésion est assurée par
la confiance, un équilibre des forces et un ensemble de valeurs communes. Ces valeurs
témoignent d'une culture d'entreprise et d'une identité qui sont tangibles, tant pour nos
clients que pour nos collaborateurs. Je pense que cet état d'esprit nous rend authentiques.

UM Merci beaucoup pour cet entretien !